KEY PRACTICES FOR FOSTERING
ENGAGED LEARNING

SERIES ON **ENGAGED LEARNING** AND **TEACHING**

Series Editors: Jessie L. Moore and Peter Felten

KEY PRACTICES FOR FOSTERING ENGAGED LEARNING

A Guide for Faculty and Staff

Jessie L. Moore

Series Foreword by Peter Felten and Jessie L. Moore

Series on Engaged Learning and Teaching

Copublished in association with

NEW YORK AND LONDON

First published in 2023 by Stylus Publishing, LLC.

Published in 2023 by Routledge
605 Third Avenue, New York, NY 10017
4 Park Square, Milton Park, Abingdon, Oxon OX14 4RN

Routledge is an imprint of the Taylor & Francis Group, an informa business.

Library of Congress Cataloging-in-Publication-Data
[to come]

ISBN: 978-1-64267-116-2 (hbk)
ISBN: 978-1-64267-117-9 (pbk)
ISBN: 978-1-00344-554-8 (ebk)

DOI: 10.4324/9781003445548

For Sylvia and Rick Moore, Jeanne and Charles Moore, and Josephine and Warren Armstrong, my first teachers

CONTENTS

SERIES FOREWORD

*K*ey Practices for Fostering Engaged Learning: A Guide for Faculty and Staff is part of the Series on Engaged Learning and Teaching, published by Stylus in partnership with the Center for Engaged Learning at Elon University. The series is designed for a multidisciplinary audience of higher education faculty, staff, graduate students, educational developers, administrators, and policymakers interested in research-informed engaged learning practices. Although individual books in the series might most appeal to those interested in a specific topic, each volume concisely synthesizes research for nonexperts and addresses the broader implications of this particular work for higher education, including effective practices for teaching, curriculum design, and educational policies. All books in the series are supplemented by open-access resources hosted on the Center for Engaged Learning's website.

Key Practices for Fostering Engaged Learning supports and extends our goals for the series. In this book, Jessie L. Moore (one of the series coeditors) synthesizes a vast body of research, including the work of more than 200 scholars who have participated in the center's multi-institutional research seminars to date, to identify six practices that are essential to high-quality engaged learning. By focusing on these cross-cutting factors, this book goes far beyond the formal list of high-impact practices to demonstrate how to transform any educational encounter into a meaningful learning experience for students in higher education. This framework makes powerful engaged learning more accessible and equitable for all students. Chapters explore each of the six key practices, drawing on cutting-edge research and concrete examples while highlighting implications for individual faculty and staff as well as for program and institutional leaders. Supplemental resources for *Key Practices for Fostering Engaged Learning*—including additional examples, discussion questions for reading groups, and professional development materials—are available at https://www.centerforengagedlearning.org/books/key-practices-for-fostering-engaged-learning/.

To learn more about the Series on Engaged Learning and Teaching, including how to propose a book, please visit https://www.centerforengagedlearning.org/publications/.

Series Editors, Peter Felten and Jessie L. Moore
Center for Engaged Learning
Elon University

ACKNOWLEDGMENTS

For the past decade, more than 200 scholars from over 120 postsecondary institutions across more than a dozen countries have taken a leap of faith to participate in multi-institutional scholarship of teaching and learning through Elon University's Center for Engaged Learning. Quite simply, this book would not exist without them, and I am grateful for the opportunities to learn with and from them as we've explored focused engaged learning topics. Each research seminar has represented a partnership with innovative coleaders: Julia Bleakney, Peter Felten, CJ Eubanks Fleming, Eric Hall, Caroline Ketcham, Deandra Little, Buffie Longmire-Avital, Cara Lucia, Shannon Lundeen, Paul Miller, Nina Namaste, Paula Rosinski, Amanda Sturgill, Maureen Vandermaas-Peeler, and Tony Weaver, of Elon; Chris Anson, North Carolina State University; Randy Bass, Georgetown University; Laura Behling, University of Puget Sound; Mimi Benjamin, Indiana University of Pennsylvania; Jody Jessup-Anger, Marquette University; W. Brad Johnson, United States Naval Academy; Jillian Kinzie, Indiana University; Judene Pretti, University of Waterloo; Neal Sobania, Pacific Lutheran University; and Michael Vande Berg, MVB Associates. The seminars also flourished thanks to the behind-the-scenes work and generous hospitality of Laura Clifton, Christopher Sulva, Sarah Williams, and Christina Wittstein.

Jason Husser and Kaye Usry, director and associate director of the Elon Poll, collaborated with the center on three national surveys referenced in this book, and Sophia Abbot helped shape the questions for the 2019 survey during her time as the center's graduate apprentice.

Elon colleagues Tim Peeples, senior associate provost for faculty affairs, and Peter Felten, the center's executive director and assistant provost for teaching and learning, have been my long-term thought-partners and advocates for the center's work. Along with Connie Book, Leo Lambert, Steven House, and the Board of Trustees of Elon University, they have championed the center's mission to facilitate multi-institutional scholarship of teaching and learning so that colleges and universities around the world can implement more equitable and just engaged learning practices.

David Brightman and John von Knorring, along with their team at Stylus Publishing, have been exceptional partners in our efforts to share this multi-institutional research, even before we launched the Series on Engaged Learning and Teaching. Milton Chambers' copyedits and Marianna Vertullo's guidance and eagle eye during production added finesse to this text. Jennie Goforth's editing and design enhanced the open-access resources available on the book's website (https://www.centerforengagedlearning.org/books/ key-practices-for-fostering-engaged-learning/); as the center's managing editor her skilled leadership across our publishing projects also gave me space to finish this book.

My disciplinary colleagues in Elon's professional writing and rhetoric program—Paula Rosinski, Li Li, Travis Maynard, and Michael Strickland—often are among my first readers, and their helpful feedback informed my revisions.

Most significantly, my parents, hiking partners, fellow adventurers, and additional critical friends for manuscript drafts—Sylvia and Rick Moore—offered instrumental support on the home front during both the many research seminar weeks and my work on this manuscript.

KEY PRACTICES FOR FOSTERING HIGH-QUALITY ENGAGED LEARNING IN HIGHER EDUCATION

Eight hours a day during a summer research program for incoming first-year students, Maya works in a molecular biology lab, growing cultures and running gels. A full-time postdoc checks in with her from time to time to double-check her techniques, and a graduate student works part-time on another branch of the principal investigator's research. Midway through the summer, a high school student, Delsin, joins the lab as part of an education, outreach, and diversity program, with his work also supervised by the postdoc. Delsin occasionally asks Maya for advice, though, when others aren't available. Typically, the lab is whisper quiet, with the exception of an occasional alarm signaling loss of power in the building. Lab members eat alone in shifts, either outside the building or in a windowless conference room. Maya talks with her faculty supervisor twice during the summer, seeking clarity on how her work fits into the lab's larger research goals but leaves both meetings feeling frustrated by her lack of understanding. At the end of the summer, she notifies the faculty supervisor that she has decided not to declare a major in molecular biology, even though she still has a strong interest in the field. Maya doesn't understand the larger purpose for the work she is doing in the lab, and she feels isolated from other lab members, especially the faculty supervisor who she thought would mentor her.

In her second year at college, Maya enrolls in a writing center theory and practice course that includes phased work in the college's writing center. Two days a week, the class has seminar-style discussions about writing studies scholarship and its applicability both to peer consulting and to the students' own writing experiences. Two additional days a week, Maya observes experienced consultants during writing center sessions and completes guided reflections about how the consultants apply writing center theory and pedagogy. As the semester progresses, Maya earns the opportunity to lead sessions under the supervision of experienced consultants, with the faculty director nearby. After each session, Maya talks with the experienced consultant about her self-assessment of the strengths and challenges of the session and makes notes about questions and ideas to raise in the next class session. For the final project in the class, Maya writes a journal article manuscript for a peer consultant column in a writing center publication, discussing drafts with peers and her faculty member before sending a revised version to the journal for review. Near the end of the semester, the faculty director invites the students to her house for a potluck dinner. Maya's manuscript receives a revise and resubmit decision after the semester has ended, but she has a community with whom to process the feedback. Excited about what she's learning, she declares a major in English so that she can continue to study professional writing, and she accepts a part-time paid consulting position in the writing center, where she continues to work until she graduates.[1]

Comparing these two experiences highlights six key practices that fostered engaged learning in Maya's second year (and that were minimally present in, or even noticeably absent from, her first-year research experience):

- Class discussions and Maya's work in the writing center acknowledged and *built on students' prior knowledge and experiences.*
- The faculty member *facilitated relationships* among students in the course and with students' near peers (e.g., more advanced peers, such as the experienced consultants) working in the writing center.
- Maya had frequent *opportunities for feedback* from peers, near peers, and the faculty director, and even received feedback from a disciplinary scholar (the journal editor).
- Maya and her peers made *connections to contexts beyond the classroom*—both to the writing center on campus and to broader disciplinary conversations.
- Maya and her peers had frequent *opportunities for guided reflection* on their learning and their own development as consultants.
- The authentic experience consulting in the writing center *promoted integration and transfer of knowledge and skills* from the course and prompted Maya to consider the discipline's relevance to her professional goals.

This book unpacks these six key practices, grounding them in relevant research and offering strategies for applying them in varied higher education contexts. As Maya's experiences highlight, opportunities for engaged learning are important in college classes but also aren't limited to the physical or virtual classroom; on-campus employment, leadership roles in student organizations, and mentored internships or undergraduate research experiences represent only a few of the many opportunities for staff and faculty to foster meaningful learning in college. As a director of an international research center on engaged learning, I've had the opportunity to work with dozens of multi-institutional, faculty/staff research teams studying engaged learning across higher education. I draw on that research for this book, distilling six strategies that continue to emerge as key practices for fostering engaged learning—across learning activities, in and beyond the classroom.

Regardless of your role on campus, you'll find examples of how to enact these practices with the students you supervise, teach, advise, or mentor. In addition, supplemental resources available on the book's website (https://www .centerforengagedlearning.org/books/key-practices-for-fostering-engaged-learning/) will help you reflect on how to adopt these six key practices in your specific context, and if you lead professional development activities for others on your campus, I've offered additional recommendations and resources for supporting colleagues' adoption of the practices.

As a foundation for exploring the six key practices, this chapter shares a definition of *engaged learning*, situates the six key practices within related scholarly conversations, and begins to explore the importance of each of these practices for fostering engaged learning in higher education.

What Is *Engaged Learning?*

Amid the myriad of learning- and learner-focused terms in higher education, this book examines engaged learning. *Engaged learning* entails students actively and intentionally participating in their own learning, not only at discrete moments but rather as an ongoing, lifelong activity. As *How People Learn II* notes, "*Learn* is an active verb; it is something people do, not something that happens to them. People are not passive recipients of learning, even if they are not always aware that the learning process is happening" (National Academies of Sciences, Engineering, and Medicine, 2018, p. 12). Similarly, Susan A. Ambrose, Michael W. Bridges, Michele DiPietro, Marsha C. Lovett, and Marie K. Norman (2010) define *learning*

> as a *process* that leads to *change*, which occurs as a result of *experience* and increases the potential for improved performance and future learning. . . . It is the direct result of how students interpret and respond to their *experiences*—conscious and unconscious, past and present. (p. 3, emphasis in the original)

While these definitions of *learning* suggest that the process can happen unconsciously, *engaged* learning adds an element of conscious, intentional, and active participation.

Student development and success scholarship, including projects like the National Survey of Student Engagement (NSSE), use *engagement* to invoke "two elements: what the student does and what the institution does" (Wolf-Wendel et al., 2009, p. 413). Building on this institutional involvement, in *Engaged Learning in the Academy: Challenges and Possibilities*, David Thornton Moore (2013) writes that effective engaged learning pedagogies

> induce the learner to look carefully at her experience, to question her own assumptions, to place the experience in relation to larger institutional and societal processes and discourses, to hear others' voices, to grapple with the question of why things happen the way they do, to imagine how things might be different, to read her experience in terms given by major social theories and to critique those theories from the perspective of her experience— to engage, in other words, in serious critical thinking. (pp. 201–202)

Even as they invite the dual contributions of students and institution (or the faculty and staff who act on behalf of the institution), these pedagogies elicit the student's active participation in her learning—as she questions, imagines, and critiques. And while students' college courses, degree programs, and cocurricular experiences often are time-bounded, institutional missions and students' own professional development goals typically reflect an intention for application or transfer of those experiences and associated knowledge to contexts beyond the university. *How People Learn II* devotes a chapter to "Learning Across the Life Span" and suggests that active engagement is particularly important for learning to occur outside of structured education or training programs.

As a result, fostering engaged learning in higher education—and giving college students opportunities to practice active and intentional participation in their learning—is critical to lifelong learning goals.

> Engaged learning entails students actively and intentionally participating in their own learning, not only at discrete moments but rather as an ongoing, lifelong activity.

How Do the Six Key Practices Extend Other Conversations About Engaged Learning?

Although other publications focus on aspects of engaged learning, including challenges associated with maintaining quality while scaling up access, providing equitable experiences for all students, and fostering integration, these texts typically do not provide extended discussions of the key practices that make teaching and learning practices high impact. The American Association of Colleges and Universities (AAC&U) has published a number of short publications that are critical contributions to our understanding of the 11 AAC&U-designated high-impact educational practices (HIPs; e.g., Brownell & Swaner, 2010; Kuh, 2008; Kuh & O'Donnell, 2013):

- capstone courses and projects
- collaborative assignments and projects
- common intellectual experiences
- diversity/global learning
- ePortfolios
- first-year seminars and experiences
- internships
- learning communities
- service-learning, community-based learning
- undergraduate research
- writing-intensive courses

These publications' brevity means that they tend to focus on case studies and outcomes, offering scarce detail (e.g., a bulleted list, a table of examples, etc.) about the essential actions for fostering high-quality engaged learning. *Key Practices for Fostering Engaged Learning* builds on, strengthens, and modifies this foundation.

George Kuh, Jillian Kinzie, John Schuh, Elizabeth Whitt, and Associates' (2005) *Student Success in College: Creating Conditions That Matter* offers more detail but focuses principally on institution-level structures and practices; five chapters focus on "effective practices used at DEEP [Documenting Effective Educational Practice] colleges and universities," but the book is now 17 years old. Over the past decade, Elon University's Center for Engaged Learning research seminars (described more in the following) and other institutional and multi-institutional research projects have extended what we know about facilitating high-quality engaged learning. Drawing from these research seminars, *Key Practices for Fostering Engaged Learning* also builds on the scholarly teaching conversation established by other significant publications on student learning. More than 2 decades ago, Arthur W. Chickering and Zelda F. Gamson (1987) wrote that "good practice in undergraduate education:"

1. Encourages contacts between students and faculty.
2. Develops reciprocity and cooperation among students.
3. Uses active learning techniques.

4. Gives prompt feedback.
5. Emphasizes time on task.
6. Communicates high expectations.
7. Respects diverse talents and ways of learning. (p. 3)

This list inspired multiple adaptations, including principles for good practice in student affairs, the Learning Process Inventory and Assessment, and the National Survey of Student Engagement (NSSE; Chickering & Gamson, 1999). Therefore, it's not surprising that Chickering and Gamson's seven principles foreshadow George Kuh's (2008) description of high-impact activities, which Kuh, Ken O'Donnell, and Carol Geary Schneider revisited in 2017 as "eight key HIPs features":

- performance expectations set at appropriately high levels
- significant investment of concentrated effort by students over an extended period of time
- interactions with faculty and peers about substantive matters
- experiences with diversity, wherein students are exposed to and must contend with people and circumstances that differ from those with which students are familiar
- frequent, timely, and constructive feedback
- opportunities to rediscover relevance of learning through real-world applications
- public demonstration of competence
- periodic structured opportunities to reflect and integrate learning (p. 11)

In this book, the six key practices for fostering engaged learning echo elements of these lists, particularly the preceding 2017 list of "key HIPs features." But the key practices also reorient attention by faculty, staff, programs, and institutions to six priorities that are based on findings from multi-institutional research seminars (described later in this chapter and in subsequent chapters) and other studies. Moreover, individual faculty and staff can enact the key practices in and beyond the classroom, regardless of whether their institution implements HIPs.

While HIPs publications focus on the educational *activities* that faculty, staff, or institutions can offer, other scholars have examined student *learning*. In *How Learning Works: 7 Research-Based Principles for Smart Teaching*, for example, Ambrose et al. (2010) identify seven principles of learning from multidisciplinary K–12 and higher education literature. Similarly the 2018 update to *How People Learn* synthesizes decades of research from multiple fields to identify 21 conclusions about learning across the lifespan (National Academies of Sciences, Engineering, and Medicine, 2018).

Table 1.1 synthesizes HIPs scholarship, learning science research, and the key practices for fostering engaged learning, which draw on a decade of international and multi-institutional research from the Center for Engaged Learning at Elon University.

TABLE 1.1
Comparing the Key Practices, High-Impact Practices Scholarship, and Learning Science Research

Key Practices for Fostering Engaged Learning	HIPs Research, and Learning Science Research
Acknowledging and building on students' prior knowledge and experiences	*HIPs:* HIPs set performance expectations at appropriately challenging levels (Kuh et al., 2017).
	Learning Science: Students' prior knowledge can help learning by reducing attentional demands or can hinder learning by causing bias, lack of attention to new information, or overreliance on that prior knowledge (Ambrose et al., 2010; National Academies of Sciences, Engineering, and Medicine, 2018).
Facilitating relationships	*HIPs:* HIPs put students in circumstances that necessitate interaction with faculty and peers (Chickering & Gamson, 1987) about substantive matters, over extended time, and expose students to people and circumstances that differ from those with which students are familiar (Kuh, 2008; Kuh et al., 2017).
	Learning Science: Although relationships are not explicitly addressed, learning often is described as a social act.
Offering feedback	*HIPs:* Frequent, timely, and constructive feedback about students' performance contributes to the "high-impact" nature of HIPs (Chickering & Gamson, 1987; Kuh, 2008; Kuh et al., 2017).
	Learning Science: Engaging students in goal-directed practice and providing targeted feedback facilitates students' learning and development of metacognitive skills (Ambrose et al., 2010; National Academies of Sciences, Engineering, and Medicine, 2018).

(Continues)

Table 1.1 (*Continued*)

Key Practices for Fostering Engaged Learning	HIPs Research, and Learning Science Research
Framing connections to broader contexts	*HIPs:* HIPs provide opportunities for students to discover the relevance of their learning through real-world applications, on and off campus (Kuh, 2008; Kuh et al., 2017).
	Learning Science: Making logical connections among information enables students to generalize their knowledge and solve problems (National Academies of Sciences, Engineering, and Medicine, 2018).
Fostering reflection on learning and self	*HIPs:* HIPs provide periodic, structured opportunities to reflect (Kuh et al., 2017).
	Learning Science: Students must attend to and adapt their approaches to learning (Ambrose et al., 2010), and that ability to self-regulate can evolve over time (National Academies of Sciences, Engineering, and Medicine, 2018).
Promoting integration and transfer of knowledge and skills	*HIPs:* HIPs provide periodic, structured opportunities to integrate learning (Kuh et al., 2017).
	Learning Science: Students need to practice integrating component skills and experiences and applying them to new contexts or challenges (Ambrose et al., 2010; National Academies of Sciences, Engineering, and Medicine, 2018). Learners' capacity to integrate changes over time and is shaped by their context and prior attempts at integration (National Academies of Sciences, Engineering, and Medicine, 2018).

Obviously, these practices, principles, and conclusions closely align. So what does this book add to the conversation? Since 2009, the Center for Engaged Learning at Elon University has facilitated multiyear, multi-institutional, and multidisciplinary research seminars on focused engaged learning topics:

- teaching democratic thinking (2009–2011)
- critical transitions: writing and the question of transfer (2011–2013)
- excellence in mentored undergraduate research (2014–2016)

- integrating global learning with the university experience: higher impact study abroad and off-campus domestic study (2015–2017)
- faculty change toward high-impact pedagogies (2016–2018)
- residential learning communities as a HIP (2017–2019)
- capstone experiences (2018–2020)
- writing beyond the university: fostering writers' lifelong learning and agency (2019–2021)
- (re)examining conditions for meaningful learning experiences (2020–2023)
- work-integrated learning (2022–2024)

As this list reflects, the center now launches a new international research seminar each year. For each seminar, we accept 20–30 higher education scholars through a competitive application process. These faculty and staff commit to collaborating on 3-year research projects, with 1-week meetings each of three consecutive summers. During summer 1, participants form multi-institutional cohorts of four to six scholars to develop shared research questions and research methods that align with the overarching seminar topic. Participants then return to their home campuses to collect their first year of data. During summer 2, cohorts analyze their year 1 data and share early results across cohorts so that participants can begin looking for intersecting themes; they also develop research plans and materials for a second year of data collection. During summer 3, participants reconvene to continue analyzing their data and share some of their findings at the Conference on Engaged Learning, held annually adjacent to whichever research seminar is in its third summer.

I've had the privilege of having a role in each of these research seminars, first as a participant, then as a seminar leader, and subsequently as the center's director, planning, implementing, and assessing each research seminar. From this perspective, I've identified six key practices prevalent across the seminars' findings—the focus of this book.

While reinforcing prior scholarly teaching conversations about student learning, these six key practices further reflect lessons learned from this multi-institutional, mixed-methods research. The center already has worked with over 200 scholars from more than a dozen different countries. Participants have represented research-intensive universities, liberal arts colleges, community colleges, and many other institutional types. As a result, research cohorts have been able to examine how what they learn about undergraduate research or study abroad or writing or other engaged learning practices applies across multiple institution types, leading to more generalizable recommendations for practice—and a more robust understanding of what adaptations might be needed to support learners in specific contexts.

Each key practices chapter in this book builds on this principle of adaptability by offering accessible overviews of relevant research and concrete strategies for faculty, staff, and institutional leaders invested in implementing high-quality engaged learning across varied institutional contexts. The book includes examples of application across all 11 HIPs and other pedagogies, and many of the examples illustrate potential intersections among these pedagogies (e.g., writing-intensive first-year experiences, collaborative assignments in capstone courses, service-learning in study away, etc.). I organize these examples as occurring *in* the physical or virtual classroom and *beyond* the classroom; although this boundary is fluid, since some course-based activities happen outside physical or virtual classroom spaces, my goal is to celebrate engaged learning practices in traditional learning contexts while also drawing increased attention to staff and faculty efforts to foster engaged learning outside of these officially designated learning spaces. Each key practices chapter ends with two sets of specific implications and recommendations tailored for individual faculty and staff and for program and institution leaders.

Why Do the Six Key Practices Need More Attention in Colleges and Universities?

Collectively, the six key practices for fostering engaged learning prepare students to actively and intentionally participate in their own learning as an ongoing, lifelong activity. Students who experience these practices will learn more during college and are better equipped to contribute to communities and workplaces beyond the university because they gain confidence identifying and applying relevant prior knowledge, working with diverse others, requesting and using feedback, making connections, and reflecting on their abilities to contribute—and on gaps in their understanding. Four of the key practices help students develop strategies for applying what they learn to both routine and new situations:

- *Acknowledging and building on students' prior knowledge and experiences* helps them learn to inventory their relevant knowledge as they encounter new experiences.
- *Facilitating relationships* helps students learn to collaborate with others.
- *Offering feedback* helps students seek and respond to feedback from others.
- *Framing connections to broader contexts* helps students develop strategies for identifying and using relevant knowledge and strategies to address the world's wicked problems.

As a result, all four key practices play pivotal roles in college learning and in preparing students for success in their careers, civic participation, and 21st-century lives. Two additional key practices amplify the impact of these practices for lifelong learning:

- *Fostering reflection and metacognition* helps students assess their own understanding of and ability to apply their relevant knowledge so that they can decide when they need to pursue additional learning.
- *Promoting integration and transfer of knowledge and skills* helps students conceptualize learning not only as happening at discrete moments in specific classes or disciplines, but rather as an ongoing, lifelong activity that requires drawing from multiple prior and concurrent contexts to select and adapt relevant knowledge and skills.

The key practices image (Figure 1.1) therefore illustrates the six practices as interlocking, centered around reflection and encircled by integration and transfer. The subsequent chapters address each of these practices in more

Figure 1.1. Key practices for fostering engaged learning.

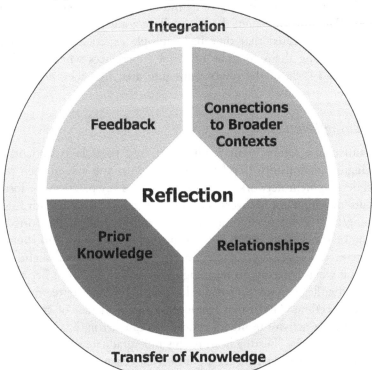

detail, and I conclude this introduction with additional discussion of why colleges and universities should give each of these practices more attention.

Acknowledging and Building on Students' Prior Knowledge and Experiences

Extending beyond Kuh's assertion that HIPs feature "performance expectations set at appropriately high levels" (Kuh, 2013, p. 8), chapter 2 examines how high-quality engaged learning builds on students' prior knowledge and experiences. Ambrose et al. (2010) remind us, "When students can connect what they are learning to accurate and relevant prior knowledge, they learn and retain more" (p. 15). Therefore making prior knowledge and experiences visible to everyone involved in the learning process and helping students practice applying or adapting that prior knowledge—with opportunities for feedback—combine to support students actively and intentionally participating in their college studies and in lifelong learning.

Although any curriculum structure with prerequisites assumes that students are using prior knowledge and experiences from those prerequisite courses in their subsequent course work, this assumption that students will transfer their learning from one context to another is not transparent to students. In a 2019 survey conducted by the Center for Engaged Learning and the Elon Poll, only 58.9% of the U.S. college graduates surveyed (n=1,575, ages 18–34) indicated that they had multiple experiences during college of faculty asking them to draw on prior experiences when they learned new things; 14.5% of the respondents indicated that they *never* had this experience.

Facilitating Relationships

Substantive interactions with faculty, staff, and peers help students form meaningful relationships (see Felten et al., 2016) and extend their professional development networks. Chapter 3 explores key practices for fostering students' development of diverse networks. In the 2019 Center for Engaged Learning/Elon Poll survey, nearly 83% of college graduates reported having one or more meaningful relationships with faculty or staff, but a full 17% never developed such a relationship. The numbers are slightly more promising when focusing on meaningful relationships with other students, as 88% of college graduates surveyed reported having one or more meaningful connections. Given that relationships are a marker of good practice or high-impact activity in higher education (Chickering & Gamson, 1987; Kuh, 2008) and the "beating heart of the undergraduate experience" (Felten & Lambert, 2020, p. 1), colleges should strive to ensure that 100% of college graduates report having multiple meaningful relationships with faculty, staff, and peers.

Offering Feedback

When faculty and staff offer constructive formative and summative feedback, students are better equipped to advance their understanding and application of key concepts. Drawing from both engaged learning and writing studies scholarship, chapter 4 offers strategies for increasing the number of substantive feedback cycles, incorporating both faculty/staff and peer feedback.

In the 2019 survey, nearly 72% of survey participants reported receiving feedback from faculty/staff on final projects multiple times, but 21% indicated they received this final feedback only once, and 7% indicated they never received feedback on a final project. Only 66% of these U.S. college graduates reported receiving feedback from faculty/staff multiple times to guide their work before they submitted a final version, and only 58% reported routinely receiving feedback from peers on work-in-progress.

Feedback is central to learning—and a critical component of professional activity in the workforce—so students need opportunities to practice asking for and acting on feedback. Yet offering timely feedback does not have to be an overwhelming task for any one faculty or staff member in a student's life if colleges develop feedback cultures. Ideally, learners develop strategies for using self-assessment, peer and near-peer feedback, and faculty/staff feedback to inform their continued practice and learning.

Framing Connections to Broader Contexts

Chapter 5 offers strategies for scaffolding students' exploration of and practice in real-world applications of their knowledge and skills. Approximately 88% of the college graduates responding to the 2019 survey indicated that they had one or more opportunities to practice real-world applications of what they were learning during their college experience. Nevertheless, in an open-response question, survey participants repeatedly expressed a desire for their college or university to have provided more learning experiences that approximated the tasks they were encountering as college graduates.

Maya's experience in her college's writing center course offers one example of how curricular and cocurricular spaces can enable students to connect their learning to authentic "real-world" tasks. Client-based projects, service-learning, study abroad, internships, and on-campus employment often foster students' connections among what they're learning and broader contexts. Chapter 5 shares strategies for framing these connections across campus contexts for learning.

Fostering Reflection on Learning and Self

Opportunities for reflection facilitate integration and transfer of learning, and opportunities for *metacognitive* reflection prepare students to take more active roles in their own learning. Chapter 6 illustrates this key practice. Only 55% of U.S. college graduates reported having multiple opportunities to reflect on how the different parts of their college experience fit together, and 17% indicated they never had opportunities for that type of reflection (Center for Engaged Learning/Elon Poll, 2019). College graduates were more likely to have had opportunities to reflect on how what they were learning would apply to their futures, with 66% reporting multiple opportunities for that reflection, and 23% reporting one opportunity for that forward-looking reflection. Chapter 6 offers concrete strategies to bolster these opportunities for reflection and metacognition across campus.

Promoting Integration and Transfer of Knowledge and Skills

Drawing from studies of integration and transfer of learning/knowledge/skills, chapter 7 illustrates how the other five key practices collectively facilitate students' connection-making among new knowledge, prior knowledge, concurrently gained knowledge from other contexts, and future goals. Higher education curricula are built on the assumption that students will transfer knowledge from course to course, particularly if courses have prerequisites or are part of a strategic course sequence within a major or minor. Yet several studies have demonstrated that neither faculty nor students expect what students learn in prior courses to be applicable to their subsequent courses (e.g., Bergmann & Zepernick, 2007; Driscoll, 2011; Nelms & Dively, 2007). And when students do try to apply knowledge from prior courses, their current faculty may not recognize students are attempting that transfer of knowledge (Nowacek, 2011). Responding to these challenges, chapter 7 shares strategies for promoting transfer and integration in and beyond the classroom—and for making students' transfer attempts more visible to faculty and staff who can offer feedback to inform students' future practice.

Key Practices for Fostering *Equitable* Engaged Learning

We cannot rely solely on officially designated HIPs to integrate engaged learning into higher education. Of the 1,575 college graduates, ages 18–34, who responded to the 2019 survey, 51.7% had an internship or work placement during college, 35.4% took part in service-learning or a community-engaged learning course, 31.7% reported having a capstone project or experience, 31.6% reported completing an independent undergraduate research project, 19.3% had a study abroad experience, and only 17.5% composed an ePortfolio. These results roughly coincide with what is reported in other large-scale studies of student experiences; for example, in the 2019 NSSE, seniors reported participating in internships, research, and study abroad at similar rates, but across Carnegie classifications, more seniors reported participating in culminating experiences (with a range of 37% to 76% depending on the institution type; NSSE, 2019a, p. 13).

Some institutions now require one or more of these HIPs, which may increase the likelihood that students at those institutions experience the beneficial outcomes associated with HIPs. Embedding the six key practices across curricular and cocurricular experiences, though, *even more equitably ensures* that students develop capacities as engaged, lifelong learners. Every faculty and staff member can embed the key practices in their courses and programs across the university, ensuring that students encounter and practice them in multiple courses and cocurricular activities, regardless of the pathways they take through their college education. Of course, you do not need to wait for a campus-wide initiative to pursue or contribute to the goal of fostering equitable, engaged learning. Chapter 8 explores additional implications of the current unequal participation in HIPs and challenges readers to adopt the six key practices to enact more equitable and just higher education. As you read the following chapters, I hope you will consider how you can apply or deepen these six key practices in your own work with students, wherever you interact with them, to foster their engaged learning.

Note

1. The student profiles at the beginning of each chapter are composites and intended to showcase a sampling of the diverse student identities and experiences represented in Center for Engaged Learning research seminar studies and in today's colleges and universities.

2

ACKNOWLEDGING AND BUILDING ON STUDENTS' PRIOR KNOWLEDGE AND EXPERIENCES

Nadia slips into a seat moments before her professor begins class, sensing his displeasure that she's still finishing her granola bar. With an 8 to 5 job, she struggles to get across town in rush hour traffic, find a parking spot, and reach the classroom in time for her 5:30 class; he'll have to put up with her granola bar since there's no time to eat dinner before or during her back-to-back evening classes. She's grateful, though, that she's been able to take evening sections of most of her required courses, since that's enabled her to keep her job as an assistant front office manager at the hotel where she's worked since graduating high school. Nadia started on the night shift as a desk clerk but quickly advanced as her supervisors noted how effectively she interacted with guests. Over the past 2 years, she'd refined the training program for new desk clerks and taken the lead on implementing a new reservation system. Yet, with a well-respected hospitality management program down the road at the university, she'd watched several recent college graduates start in the front office manager position and move on to other opportunities, making it clear that she needed to earn a BS if she wanted to advance within the company.

Nadia had looked forward to the Guest Service Management course, anticipating that her job experience would be relevant. Unfortunately, her professor seems to prefer textbook examples over real-world experience. Several days she's come to class eager to talk about how she's used a guest service assessment strategy or how she's helped establish a guest service culture, but there's never an opportunity to share her experience beyond a few small-group discussions. She's not sure her professor even knows she's worked in hospitality for 6 years! Thank goodness she's also taking Lodging Operations and Management, later in the evening. Each time the class discusses a new topic, the professor invites students to share prior experiences that might be relevant—either as part of class discussions or as short exit writes that the professor responds to at the start of the next class. Nadia appreciates these opportunities to test her application of theory to her own past and current practices; they make her long days more bearable and the challenges of being a full-time employee and part-time student more worthwhile.

Why Acknowledging and Building on Prior Knowledge and Experiences Matters

To actively and intentionally participate in their lifelong learning—that is, to be engaged learners—students must be able to identify their relevant prior knowledge and experiences ("the prior") and adapt them for new contexts. And college staff and faculty play a key role in helping students learn strategies to inventory their prior knowledge and to repurpose it successfully. Discussions of high-impact educational practices (HIPs) often allude to this cornerstone practice for fostering engaged learning. In "Taking HIPs to the Next Level," for instance, George Kuh (2013) asserts that HIPs feature "performance expectations set at appropriately high levels" (p. 8; see also Kuh et al., 2017). Establishing appropriate expectations requires understanding what prior knowledge and experiences students bring to the learning situation. And facilitating students' intentional participation in their learning— a hallmark of engaged learning—necessitates teaching students to take stock of their prior knowledge and experiences so that they intentionally can self-assess the prior's relevancy to new learning situations. As a result, acknowledging and building on students' prior knowledge, the focus of this chapter, is a cornerstone for the other key practices for fostering engaged learning (see Figure 2.1).

In the 2019 Center for Engaged Learning/Elon Poll of recent college graduates, only 58.9% reported faculty repeatedly asking them to draw on prior experiences when they learned new things, and 26.6% reported encountering that invitation to call on their prior experiences only once during their college careers; 14.5% reported never being asked to explicitly draw on the knowledge they brought to a course from their other coursework and life experiences. Why does this gap matter?

Figure 2.1. Prior knowledge as a cornerstone for fostering engaged learning.

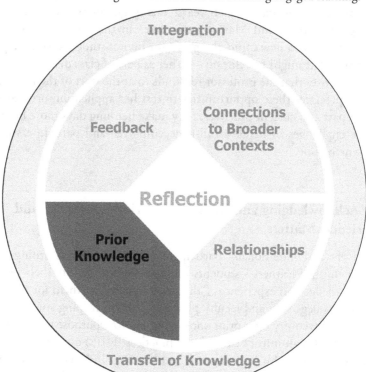

Understanding and building on students' prior knowledge and experiences underpins teaching and learning. As Ambrose et al. (2010) highlight in one of their seven principles for teaching, "Students' prior knowledge can help or hinder learning" (p. 13). Prior knowledge can help learning—if students draw on it—by reducing the amount of conscious attention students need to spend on the familiar or routinized part of a concept or activity, allowing students instead to focus on what's new and potentially challenging (Ambrose et al., 2010; National Academies of Sciences, Engineering, and Medicine, 2018). Prior knowledge can hinder learning, though, if students try to apply irrelevant prior knowledge or if their application of "the prior" interferes with their ability to prioritize new information or to recognize key, distinguishing aspects of new problems (Ambrose et al., 2010; National Academies of Sciences, Engineering, and Medicine, 2018). Scholars in the Center for Engaged Learning's research seminars reaffirm the importance of prior knowledge and experiences in fostering engaged learning and extend the discussion in important ways.

When we view engaged learning as students actively participating in their own learning, not only at discrete moments but rather as an ongoing, lifelong activity, we need to think of "the prior" as:

- inclusive of students' dispositions, values, and beliefs
- recursive, informing not only the current learning moment but also continually (re)shaped by learners' experiences in and beyond the classroom
- hidden, unless we make conscious efforts to make "the prior" visible for learners, teachers, supervisors, and others

Nadia's prior knowledge includes her actual work experience, of course, but it also includes her assumption that her work experience should be relevant to her coursework and her belief that college degrees helped her colleagues advance more quickly. She's eager to discuss her experiences with peers and faculty and seems open to applying what she's learning in her classes to her current work setting. Yet her prior experience remains hidden in her Guest Service Management class, making it impossible for her professor to help her gauge what parts of her prior knowledge are helping and what parts might be hindering her learning. As a result, the class represents a missed opportunity to foster engaged learning. In contrast, her Lodging Operations and Management instructor seeks to make students' prior knowledge visible (e.g., to activate it), enabling everyone in the class to actively participate in assessing whether their prior knowledge is sufficient, appropriate, and accurate—and to build on the prior to deepen class discussions and student learning.

Like Nadia, approximately 5 million U.S. college students are adult learners (25 or older) who are enrolled part-time (Renn & Reason, 2021). Hussar and Bailey (2019) project that by 2027, approximately 23% of college students will be 25–34 and approximately 16% will be 35 or older. Part-time enrollment (across age groups) is projected to reach 8.1 million students by 2027 (Hussar & Bailey, 2019). Moreover, while many college curricula assume that students follow "traditional" enrollment patterns, entering college directly from high school and completing their degree in 4 years, U.S. national statistics tell a different story. Renn and Reason (2021) report that less than half of the first-time bachelor degree earners who graduated from college in 2015–2016 completed their degrees in 4 years. And based on their synthesis of recent research, they describe the variety of U.S. undergraduates:

> College students in the United States engage in nonlinear attendance patterns; take courses (or entire degrees) online; attend for-profit institutions; come from underrepresented racial, ethnic, and/or religious groups; speak a first language other than English; work between high school and college;

work 30-plus hours a week *during* college; are international students; raise families; negotiate accommodations for disabilities; and/or do not complete their intended educational goals. (pp. vii–viii)

This tremendous variation makes it difficult to anticipate what prior knowledge students bring to each learning experience—and makes it all the more important to make prior knowledge visible so that students and their faculty/staff can build on it.

During the 2011–2013 Center for Engaged Learning research seminar, 45 international scholars studied writing transfer—how writers (successfully) take what they learn about writing in one context and adapt it for other contexts with different expectations. Chapter 7 takes a closer look at transfer of learning, but in this chapter, I'll highlight what teams have reported about the role of the prior in student learning about writing, informing two of the essential principles about writing transfer.

The first writing transfer principle related to prior knowledge and experiences states, "Students' dispositions (e.g., habits of mind) and identities inform the success of their unique writing transfer experiences" (Moore, 2017, p. 7). Alison Farrell, Sandra Kane, Cecilia Dube, and Steve Salchak (2017), for example, surveyed incoming students at their colleges in Ireland, South Africa, and the United States to understand what writing experience students bring from high school to college. Their research attends to what Alexander Astin (1993) has labeled *inputs* in his IEO model—inputs (I), the college environment (E), and outputs (O). Astin's framework advocates that studies of college-level learning and teaching can't attend only to what happens in college; to understand the effect or outcomes of specific pedagogical strategies or institutional initiatives, scholars also need to understand how students' characteristics and precollege experiences inform their interactions in and with the college environment. Inputs aren't synonymous with prior knowledge and experiences, but they are an aspect of the prior that often is measured and tracked in national surveys.

Farrell et al. focus on a specific type of input—students' writing experiences in high school—and Table 2.1 highlights findings from their study. As Farrell et al. (2017) write,

Data from all three sites strongly suggest that the students surveyed are generally optimistic about writing and enjoy writing. The majority of them are confident about writing, but this confidence does not necessarily translate in either their *perception* of their preparedness or their *actual* preparedness. (p. 87)

TABLE 2.1
College Writing Preparedness and Success Study

University of Johannesburg	*National University of Ireland, Maynooth*	*George Washington University*
(470 students surveyed)	**(250 students surveyed)**	**(63 students surveyed)**
"I am a writer"		
49%	76%	67%
Confident about ability to write at the university level		
71%	72%	84%
Enjoy writing		
56%	89%	61%
Writing is relevant to own life		
72%	62%	67%
Completed six or more short papers (<5 pages) in final year of high school		
78%	84%	93%
Completed one or more longer papers in final year of high school		
19%	95%	88%
High school prepared them well for writing in college		
78%	59%	77%

Note. From Farrell et al., 2017.

This example illustrates the complexity of building on prior knowledge and experience; while the students at the three sites are similarly confident about their ability to write in college, they bring varied prior experience to the task. It would be a mistake, for example, to assume that all entering first-year students have experience writing longer papers of five or more pages. To effectively build on students' prior knowledge, faculty must first take time to learn about the relevant prior knowledge each new group of students brings to a course.

The second writing transfer principle states, "Successful writing transfer requires transforming or repurposing prior knowledge (even if only slightly) for a new context to adequately meet the expectations of new audiences and fulfill new purposes for writing" (Moore, 2017, p. 4). Gwen Gorzelsky, Carol Hayes, Ed Jones, and Dana Lynn Driscoll (2017) studied students' transitions from first-year writing courses to writing in the disciplines. They found that students who approached understandings of genre—or types of writing—as adaptable had greater success in their disciplinary writing, while students who approached genre as formulaic—often using prior knowledge from high school that they hadn't reshaped during first-year writing courses—were less successful in their disciplinary writing. In other words, students needed both to adapt their prior knowledge from high school coursework to accommodate more complex understandings of genre introduced in first-year writing *and* approach their evolving understanding of specific types of writing as structures that also could, and should, be adapted for new writing contexts.

Of course, to adapt prior knowledge for a new situation, students need appropriate, or relevant, prior knowledge. Elizabeth Wardle partnered with Nicolette Mercer Clement (2017) to study Nicolette's attempts to transfer writing knowledge as she advanced through her degree program. They describe a scenario in which Nicolette's writing for an honors seminar assignment was unsuccessful not because of lack of prior *writing* knowledge, but rather because her lack of prior *content* knowledge compromised her ability to write about the assigned topic. Her instructors had assumed that all students were entering the course with equivalent prior content knowledge. For Nicolette, however, terms and concepts that were assumed to be shared knowledge were new knowledge. Moreover, her lack of prior content knowledge compromised her application of prior writing knowledge since her attention was focused on making sense of new-to-her content (Wardle & Mercer Clement, 2016/2017). Nicolette's experience demonstrates the importance of making visible what prior knowledge and experiences students bring (or don't bring) to a class to create a more effective, equitable, and just foundation for learning.

Acknowledging and Building On Prior Knowledge in the Classroom

Fortunately, a number of strategies exist to make students' prior knowledge visible and to invite students to build on it. Ambrose et al. (2010), for example, suggest giving students a low-stakes assessment at the start of the semester, asking students to self-assess their prior knowledge against a list of concepts faculty expect them to bring to a course, or inviting students to create a concept map about what they know related to a topic. In their discussion of inclusive teaching practices, Tracie Marcella Addy, Derek Dube, Khadijah A. Mitchell, and Mallory E. SoRelle (2021) share a "Who's in Class?" form "that provides a venue for students to voluntarily and anonymously describe aspects about themselves that can impact how they learn in a course" (p. 139). Several of the form items would make visible at least some of students' prior knowledge and experiences. For Nadia, for example, the form would give her an opportunity to disclose her work experience and positionality as an adult learner.

Carol Van Zile-Tamsen, Janet Bean, Christina Beaudoin, David Lewis, and Tania von der Heidt (2023), participants in the 2018–2020 research seminar on capstone experiences, describe an integrative ePortfolio initiative at one of their campuses (University at Buffalo), highlighting its potential to inventory students' prior knowledge. All students are required to select completed assignments from their general education coursework; they work with mentors to "reflect on their learning experiences and select and connect artifacts that best exemplify their achievement of UB Curriculum learning outcomes" (Van Zile-Tamsen et al., 2023, p. 79). Instructors interviewed by the research team emphasize that the ePortfolio makes student learning from general education courses visible—to the student, the ePortfolio mentor, other faculty and staff with whom the student shares their ePortfolio, and the institution—as students are completing the upper-level course requirements in their majors.

While the University at Buffalo example focuses on students' prior learning from their general education courses, faculty also should be attentive to the prior knowledge and experiences students bring from internships or practicums, their involvement in student or community organizations, student employment, and other life experiences. Unearthing this prior knowledge can be as simple as facilitating a 5- to 10-minute class discussion on the following questions:

- If you've completed an internship, practicum, or similar work placement, what have you learned from your experience that might be applicable to this topic/project/class?
- What experiences from your involvement in student or community organizations seem connected to what we're learning in this class?
- If you work—whether on or off campus—what responsibilities or tasks have you had at work that seem relevant to this discussion/project?

Students may assume their prior knowledge from these contexts isn't relevant or valued, so they may not consciously draw on it. Or they may try to draw on prior knowledge that they do not realize is inappropriate or irrelevant to the current learning activity; inviting students to share prior knowledge and experiences from these realms beyond the classroom makes it possible to offer feedback on the appropriateness and accuracy of that prior knowledge for the current context.

Acknowledging and Building on Prior Knowledge Beyond the Classroom

When we think of the prior as recursive, informing not only the current learning moment, but also continually (re)shaped by learners' experiences in and *beyond* the classroom, we open up the potential to help students engage with their prior knowledge across these spaces.

Building on Prior Knowledge and Experiences in Global Learning

Participants in the 2015–2017 research seminar on Integrating Global Learning with the University Experience reaffirmed the importance of drawing on prior knowledge in study abroad and off-campus domestic study. In the *Elon Statement on Global Learning*, they issued the following charge: "Effective educators should take into account how learners' prior global experiences impact learning in subsequent opportunities" (Center for Engaged Learning, 2017, para. 12). The participants also offer insight into the types of prior knowledge and experience that global learning could draw on.

In a multi-institutional study facilitated by the research seminar, Iris Berdrow, Rebecca Cruise, Ekaterina Levintova, Sabine Smith, Laura Boudon, Dan Paracka, and Paul M. Worley (2020) surveyed students at six universities to understand student choice patterns related to global learning experiences. Focusing on 2014/2015 graduating seniors, they surveyed 382 graduates (across all six institutions) who had participated in study abroad during college and 331 graduates (across five of the institutions) who had not studied abroad. Looking at correlations between studying abroad, taking a global learning course, and participation in other global learning experiences, students who studied abroad were more likely than their peers who had not studied abroad to

- speak another language
- take a language course for fun
- participate in intercultural clubs on campus
- participate in intercultural events in the community
- live with a host family abroad
- travel internationally before college (Berdrow et al., 2020)

Similarly, students who took a global learning course were more likely than their peers who had not taken a global learning course to

- speak another language
- participate in intercultural clubs and events on campus

- participate in intercultural events in the community
- travel internationally before college

Based on these correlations, the research team suggests, "Students who are global learners show a pattern of participation, often choosing a variety of global learning experiences. . . . Once students are exposed to global content on campus, they are more likely to continue on the global learning trajectory" (pp. 67–68). While faculty and staff shouldn't assume that all learners in their study abroad programs or global learning courses have had all of these prior experiences, Berdrow et al.'s research could function as the foundation for a preexperience survey. In addition to the six prior global learning experiences listed previously, a preexperience survey could invite students to share any other prior interests and experiences they identify as relevant to their global learning.

The same research team also examined why students opted not to study abroad (Levintova et al., 2020). While participants often cited programmatic (e.g., course requirements for a major) and financial factors as hindrances to studying abroad, the team noted that several personal reasons also came into play. For example, for some participants, military affiliation had given students prior travel experiences—though not always positive experiences— which might have diminished the students' perceived valuing of additional experiences abroad. Yet, if made visible, campus educators still could invite students to draw on this prior knowledge and experience in on-campus contexts for global learning.

Building on Prior Knowledge and Experiences in Undergraduate Research

In their study of the salient practices of effective undergraduate research (UR) mentors, a research team from the 2014–2016 research seminar on Excellence in Mentoring Undergraduate Research highlighted the importance of what they call "strategic pre-planning" (Shanahan et al., 2015). Walkington et al. (2018) write:

> Effective UR mentors invest time early in the process for project selection and planning, including thinking through the kinds of research questions and tasks that are suited to undergraduates and setting achievable timelines for them. Such early planning offers the opportunity to consider the wide variability in students' levels of preparation, motivation, and skills, and to customize research roles accordingly. (p. 107)

In other words, mentored UR isn't one size fits all; mentors should ask students about their interests in the research project and about the prior knowledge and experiences that students think they could bring to a research task. This preplanning helps students find a good-fit research project and increases their likelihood of success with the research by helping mentors identify what instruction and supports they might need. Looking back at Maya's initial experience with UR (in chapter 1), her principal investigator likely did not take time for strategic preplanning to identify gaps in her prior knowledge that challenged her ability to make sense of how her piece of the research project aligned with the lab's goals.

Building on Prior Knowledge and Experiences in Student Employment

Staff who supervise student employees also can help students develop reflective habits to build on their prior knowledge. Iowa GROW® offers a rich example of inviting student employees to reflect on what prior knowledge could inform their current work—and what work experiences could inform their class-based learning and future employment (Hansen & Hoag, 2018). Conversations using the Iowa GROW model center on four questions:

1. How is this job fitting in with your academics?
2. What are you learning here that's helping you in school?
3. What are you learning in class that you can apply here at work?
4. Can you give me a couple of examples of things you've learned here that you think you'll use in your chosen profession?

These questions center an assumption that students should have relevant experiences in both their academics and in their campus employment that they can apply or adapt for the other context, and they explicitly invite students to discuss the sufficiency, appropriateness, and accuracy of that prior knowledge (Ambrose et al., 2010) for application in other contexts with their supervising staff.

Once this prior knowledge is visible, George S. McClellan, Kristina Creager, and Marianna Savoca (2018) suggest that supervisors create student employment learning goals that build on that prior. They further highlight how Bloom's taxonomy offers a framework for scaffolding students' cognitive processing from remembering and understanding to evaluating and creating as students develop additional knowledge in their on-campus employment and concurrent learning spaces.

Implications and Recommendations for Individual Faculty and Staff

Whether working with students in courses, on-campus employment, or other engaged learning contexts, individual faculty and staff can encourage students to reflect on prior knowledge and experience that might be relevant. Faculty and staff might ask:

- What have you done before that you think would be similar to what you're being asked to do for this assignment or project?
- What strategies did you use successfully for that task?
- What might you need to do differently?

Of course, as the study of entering college students' writing experiences demonstrates, sometimes students' perceptions of their prior knowledge do not match their actual preparation, so we also should think about students' prior knowledge (and gaps in their prior experiences) as we plan engaged learning opportunities. We should ask:

- Based on prior experiences with students or conversations with current students, what shared knowledge/experiences do students typically bring to my class, office/program, or research team?
- What have students struggled with in the past that I could better scaffold when I introduce this assignment or task? What am I consistently commenting on? What "trips up" the majority of my students in this course or campus context?
- If there are prerequisites for my course, what learning outcomes are students likely to have met by taking that prior course? How will I gauge their proficiency with those topics to determine which they might need to practice more?
- If the on-campus employment I supervise has required qualifications for student hires, how have I assessed that prior knowledge or experience?

Implications and Recommendations for Program and Institution Leaders

Programs and institutions can support individual faculty and staff efforts by tracking and sharing information about students' prior experiences. Within a degree program, for example, faculty could collaborate on curriculum mapping, identifying which required and elective courses typically introduce or reinforce key concepts and experiences. Curriculum mapping descriptively traces what's taught and when, but the map also can track when learners encounter specific activities or pedagogies (English, 1978, 1980; Robley et al., 2005). Such mappings allow faculty to more accurately anticipate what prior knowledge students bring to their classes based on the coursework they've already completed. (Of course, faculty need to remember that some students may be taking courses in a different sequence than anticipated or may have transferred credit for some coursework from other institutions.) Curriculum mapping also helps faculty identify potential gaps in their degree programs, such as revealing that key concepts aren't covered anywhere in the curriculum or that students haven't been introduced to key experiences before they take courses in which they are expected to practice those experiences (without the benefit of foundational instruction).

As university databases and e-systems become more advanced, institutions also should consider how to use existing tools to make students' prior knowledge and experiences more visible. At Elon University, registrar Rodney Parks and assistant registrar Casey Hayes generate learner profiles of students taking capstone seminars in the general education curriculum. These reports "illustrated the distribution of completed courses by students enrolled in each capstone, enabling the instructor to further tailor their multidisciplinary approach by knowing the disciplines in which their students excel or may require additional focus" (Parks & Hayes, 2019, para. 3). A report could show, for instance, that most of the students enrolled in a section have taken introductory psychology or that only a handful of students have taken advanced science courses. Future iterations of a learner profile also could integrate the types of information included on experiential transcripts, such as whether students have studied abroad, completed internships, or participated in UR.

Acknowledging and building on students' prior knowledge and experiences is a key practice for fostering students' active and intentional participation in their own lifelong learning. When college faculty and staff demonstrate that they value the knowledge and experiences students bring with them and help students assess the potential relevancy of that prior knowledge, they create a cornerstone for other key practices for engaged learning.

3

FACILITATING
RELATIONSHIPS

Before his senior year of high school, Delsin participated in an education, outreach, and diversity summer program at the state university, 3 hours away from his home on the reservation. He worked a few hours each day in a molecular biology lab, alongside Maya, an incoming first-year student (introduced in chapter 1), and took a couple of courses that the program offered in core subjects and in college preparation. Delsin had been nervous about being so far from home, but his peer mentor, Coburn, helped mitigate those nerves as they talked about shared experiences on the reservation and ways Coburn had stayed connected with his reservation friends and family during his first year at the university. When Delsin enrolled at the university the following year, Coburn continued to act as a guide, introducing Delsin to his friends and encouraging him to join a student organization, Keepers of the Fire. His new KOF friends were like his university family, and the organization's advisor was a bit like an uncle—letting the students have space to experiment, but also available to share advice gained from his own experience navigating the reservation to university transition, successfully graduating a few years ago, and eventually returning to the university in a staff role.

Despite these meaningful relationships, Delsin's first semester on campus has been difficult. His biology and chemistry classes both had over 200 students; it was easy to hide, and he didn't think the professors would even notice if he didn't attend. Labs were a little better because the lab instructors could learn more students' names, and his lab partners were familiar faces each week, even though they rarely talked about anything other than the current lab assignment. In contrast, Delsin's interactions with his peers and faculty in his first-year interdisciplinary seminar seemed to spill beyond the classroom; he knew most of his classmates' names because his professor used them and encouraged students to address each other by name, too. Sure, they'd needed name cards the first few weeks, but now they only used them if a guest speaker was coming to class. The professor even invited the class to a picnic at his house next week. While he was hesitant to ask for more of the professor's time, Delsin hoped the picnic would give him a chance to ask additional questions about the professor's research and whether the professor ever mentored undergraduate researchers.

Why Facilitating Relationships Matters

Relationships are a cornerstone to engaged learning, as Figure 3.1 illustrates. They foster a sense of belonging, contributing to retention and degree completion; they strengthen feedback cultures (discussed in chapter 4), supporting lifelong and lifewide learning; and they often facilitate connections to broader contexts (discussed in chapter 5). In *Relationship-Rich Education*, Peter Felten and Leo Lambert (2020) identify "four interlocking relationship-rich principles that guide both effective programs and generative cultures at college and universities," including "every student must develop a web of significant relationships" (p. 17). Substantive interactions with faculty, staff, and peer mentors help students form meaningful relationships (see Felten & Lambert, 2020; Felten et al., 2016), and those meaningful relationships have the potential to support students' academic, social, cultural, and career-focused learning and development. Friendship networks can inform academic and social development (McCabe, 2016). Meaningful interactions with faculty and peers can support students' learning outcomes (Swaner & Brownell, 2008) and contribute to the "high-impact" nature of educational practices like first-year seminars, capstone experiences, learning communities, service-learning, and undergraduate research (UR; Brownell & Swaner, 2010). And these collective relationships extend students' professional development networks.

Highlighting results from a 2018 Center for Engaged Learning/Elon Poll survey of college graduates, Lambert, Jason Husser, and Felten (2018) write, "Graduates who had seven to 10 significant relationships with faculty and staff were more than three times as likely to report their college experience as 'very rewarding' than those with no such relationships. Similar effects were found for peer relationships in college" (para. 5). Although participants in the 2018 poll overwhelmingly identified faculty as having the biggest impact on their lives during college, research from the 2017–2019 Center for Engaged Learning research seminar on residential learning communities demonstrates that staff also play a significant role in building relationship-rich college communities. Social interactions with staff and faculty are a strong predictor

Figure 3.1. Relationships as a cornerstone for fostering engaged learning.

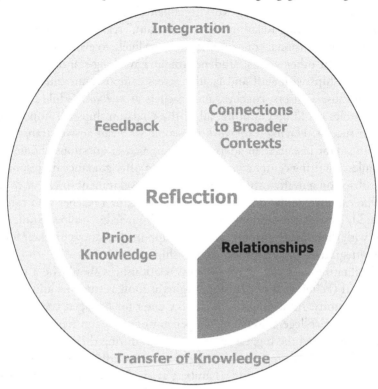

of psychological sense of community in college (Sriram, Weintraub, et al., 2020), and when considering social interactions (as opposed to academic interactions), students do not differentiate between staff and faculty roles (Sriram, Haynes, Cheatle, et al., 2020).

Staff and faculty relationships with students take a variety of forms, including on-campus employment supervisor, student organization advisor, coach, religious and spiritual life leader, academic advisor, and teacher. Sometimes, significant relationships in students' lives on campus don't come with titles that designate their contributions to students' relationship-rich education. For instance, students often develop meaningful relationships with dining hall staff and facilities staff assigned to their residence halls, yet these staff members' titles rarely signal their recurring conversations with students about daily challenges and life goals.

In his scholarship on mentoring, W. Brad Johnson (2016) highlights three categories of these roles—advisor, supervisor, and faculty sponsor—as developmental relationships "intended to enhance a junior person's career development or institutional experience" with potential for "movement from a transactional to transformational structure, low to high social support, and tentative to strong working alliance" over time (pp. 28–29). In Johnson's "Mentoring Relationship Continuum," relationships that advance along these dimensional continuums are more likely to evolve into relational mentoring. In other words, students might have long-standing, meaningful relationships with staff and faculty across campus units but count only a few of those advisors, coaches, and teachers as *mentors*. While privileging mentor roles could be tempting, all of these relationships are important to student success. Having a network of people who can answer transactional questions—for instance, an advisor who can answer questions about course schedules, a writing center consultant who can offer guidance on responding to feedback on a draft, a student professional development or career counselor who can give guidance on updating a résumé, or a teacher who can help unmuddy new-to-the-student, troublesome knowledge—allows students to focus with their faculty/staff mentors on support that draws on their longer-term, integrative, and reciprocal relationships.

Facilitating an array of meaningful relationships should be a campus-wide effort (Felten et al., 2016) that begins as soon as students join the campus community. According to the 2018 Center for Engaged Learning/Elon Poll survey of college graduates, "79 percent of graduates reported meeting the peers who had the biggest impact on them during their first year of college. And 60 percent reported meeting their most influential faculty or staff mentors during that first year" (Lambert et al., 2018, para. 6). For Delsin, that relationship-building began even before he formally matriculated, and although his sense of community could have faltered during his first year, his peers, near peers (e.g., slightly more experienced peers, such as a college senior in relation to a first-year student or a recent alum in relation to a college senior), staff, and faculty all played roles in his academic and social development.

Delsin's experience also exemplifies the significance of peer relationships. In her study of undergraduate friendship networks, Janice McCabe documented friends offering both instrumental support (e.g., studying together, reminding each other about deadlines) and emotional support. McCabe (2016) describes three types of friend networks:

- tight-knitters—dense networks in which almost all the members know each other
- compartmentalizers—clusters of smaller networks, with few connections among networks
- samplers—disconnected friendships in which the core student might be the only connection among their friends

None of these networks is better than the others. Rather, knowing that students have different experiences building their peer networks (and presumably, their networks with faculty and staff) allows colleges to think strategically about designing spaces and programs that foster development of each of these types of relationship networks—and about how to facilitate students' meaningful interactions with diverse others. That attention to diversity in peer relationships is especially important for staff and faculty working with first-generation students and students of color, who may be less satisfied with their peer interactions, particularly at predominantly white institutions (Sriram, Haynes, Weintraub, et al., 2020). Delsin, for example, likely is a tight-knitter, but the in- and out-of-class experiences associated with his first-year interdisciplinary seminar thoughtfully and intentionally connect him to an additional peer cluster.

Learning during college how to foster these types of relationships contributes to graduates' postcollege success. In the 2019 Center for Engaged Learning/Elon Poll survey, approximately 67% of recent college graduates indicated that connecting with people from different cultural backgrounds is very important or somewhat important to their day-to-day life, and 70% suggested that working with a team to accomplish goals is very or somewhat important to their day-to-day life. Employers agree; repeated studies reaffirm that employers value graduates' ability to work with others from different cultures and to collaborate on team projects (see, e.g., Finley, 2021). Unfortunately, 30% of respondents to the 2019 survey thought they had not developed skills in college for connecting with diverse others and 25% reported they had not developed teamwork skills.

Facilitating Relationships in the Classroom

In a review of scholarship on faculty–student relationships, Elin Meyers Hoffman (2014) reaffirms that positive interactions with faculty can support students' persistence at college, their academic achievement, and their personal development. When students identify as having a positive relationship with their instructor, they also may be more likely to have confidence in their ability to succeed in the class, even in difficult courses (Micari & Pazos, 2012). Even informal academic discussions, including those immediately before or after classes or during office hours, positively correlate with students' confidence and motivation (Hoffman, 2014).

One step toward facilitating relationships in the classroom is calling on students by name—and encouraging them to do the same in their interactions with peers. Although this strategy might seem second nature in small classes, calling on students by name understandably is more daunting in larger classes. Fortunately, research by Katelyn M. Cooper, Brian Haney, Anna Krieg, and Sara E. Brownell (2017) suggests that using name tents to facilitate addressing students by name still leads to relationship gains. Cooper et al. (2017) studied a high-enrollment biology class in which instructors used active-learning strategies and asked students to use name tents—folded card stock on which students wrote their names. At the end of the semester, the instructors could name approximately half of their students when looking at a deidentified photo roster, but 78% of the students surveyed thought the instructors knew their names (Cooper et al., 2017, see statistics on p. 5). Moreover 23% of the students indicated that instructors knowing their names contributed to student–instructor relationships (Cooper et al., 2017, p. 7). Tracie Marcella Addy, Derek Dube, Khadijah A. Mitchell, and Mallory E. SoRelle (2021) link this practice to creating a welcoming, inclusive classroom, noting that correctly pronouncing names and using students' pronouns further enhances inclusion.

Another low-investment strategy to foster relationships in the classroom is to check in with students not only about their understanding of course content but also about their well-being and out-of-class activities. Christina Naegeli Costa and Lauren Mims (2021), for example, describe using notecards to check in with students as a way to build rapport; they distribute blank index cards to students and ask them to select a question from two or three options written on the board and to write a brief response. Rather than focusing on course content—although that's also a great exit write strategy to check in on students' content comprehension or questions about assignments—the prompts ask about students' stress levels, self-care plans, or recent good news. Exit writes like these—very brief writing activities that students complete as an "exit ticket" at the end of class—typically aren't graded, but they provide a timely check-in with students. Costa and Mims respond either individually to students or with synthesized responses to the class. When appropriate, they include information about relevant campus resources.

Faculty also can help students build their relationship networks by integrating group work into class and introducing collaboration strategies. In the United States, students spend years navigating educational systems that privilege individual achievement, and they continue to earn individual grades for college courses at most postsecondary institutions. Working collaboratively breaks this norm, so students need instruction and practice in working with a team. Rebecca Pope-Ruark (2012) describes using Scrum, adapted from web software development, to manage collaborative projects and equip students with adaptable strategies for group work. In Scrum, teams identity project chunks for smaller groups or individual members to work on, but rather than dividing and conquering until right before the deadline, teams check in frequently—sometimes daily. In these recurring sessions, team members share updates, ask questions, solicit feedback, and collaboratively troubleshoot. As a result, even as individual students take the lead on sections of a project, the entire team knows the status of each section and can help respond to challenges, minimizing the chances of surprises as project deadlines near. In addition to facilitating relationships, project management strategies like Scrum give students opportunities to practice giving and responding to peer feedback (discussed more in chapter 4).

Facilitating Relationships Beyond the Classroom

Faculty and staff also play important roles in helping students develop relationships beyond the classroom. Several relationship-rich high-impact educational practices—mentored UR, internships, service-learning, and others—extend beyond the classroom. Yet students also spend significant portions of their days participating in student organizations, on-campus employment, and other potentially relationship-rich activities. Therefore, campus initiatives to facilitate relationships shouldn't overlook these spaces.

Facilitating Relationships in Mentored Undergraduate Research

Participants in the 2014–2016 Center for Engaged Learning research seminar on excellence in mentoring UR documented the significant roles both faculty and peers occupy in UR. Jenny Olin Shanahan, Elizabeth Ackley, Eric Hall, Kearsley Stewart, and Helen Walkington drew from an extensive review of the literature and interviews with award-winning mentors to identify 10 salient practices of UR mentors (Hall et al., 2018; Shanahan et al., 2015, 2017; Walkington et al., 2018). Several salient practices by faculty mentors help foster relationships:

- investing ongoing time in the mentor–mentee relationship, beginning with preplanning and continuing through to teaching relevant skills and to sharing findings at conferences and in publications
- balancing research expectations with appropriate emotional support
- developing community among undergraduate researchers
- creating opportunities for peer and near-peer mentoring (see also https://www.CenterForEngagedLearning.org/SalientPractices/)

These strategies for effective mentoring can amplify the outcomes of mentored UR (e.g., academic achievement, retention, communication skills), especially for historically underrepresented minority students (Shanahan, 2018). As another seminar team explored, mentored UR can support academic, professional, personal, and cultural identity development (Palmer et al., 2018), particularly when mentors attend to their mentees as individuals, not merely to the research project.

Extending this potential to support a strong mentored relationship between a faculty/staff member and a student, the salient practices also point to the potential to foster relationships among students. Ruth Palmer, Andrea Hunt, Michael Neal, and Brad Wuetherick (2018), another 2014–2016 research seminar team, note, "Although many [UR] students identified relationships with faculty mentors, they also identified other important relationships, including collaborations, working within teams, and networking with others" (p. 26). Across disciplines as Shanahan et al. (2015) highlight in their salient practices, mentors can "create intentional, laddered opportunities for peers and 'near peers' to learn mentoring skills and to bring larger numbers of undergraduates into scholarly opportunities" (p. 4). Delsin's and Maya's experiences in the molecular biology lab (in chapter 1), however, demonstrate that these opportunities must be *intentional*. Creating opportunities for students to work in proximity to each other is not the same as integrating opportunities for them to discuss their slices of the team's project, teach each other research skills and strategies, and reflect together on how their UR experiences draw on their coursework and other prior experiences—and prepare them for future goals.

While research teams might be most common in the social and natural sciences, even arts and humanities research can integrate laddered mentoring. In my disciplinary home department, for instance, students can join a research team that studies the writing lives of students and alumni. Students initially contribute to literature reviews and data analysis, with more experienced student members teaching newer team members strategies for searching the library databases or sharing our coding strategies in Dedoose, a program for collaboratively analyzing qualitative and mixed-methods data. As students become more familiar with the research, they often take ownership of analyzing and presenting on a slice of the data or propose follow-up research. Students-as-partners frameworks can help forefront intentionality in these laddered opportunities for peer and near-peer mentoring in this type of research team by elevating the importance of shared goal setting, coinquiry, and reciprocity (Abbot et al., 2020; Moore et al., 2020).

The 2014–2016 research seminar scholars amplified the potential of UR comentoring models, one type of mutual mentoring that can occur in research teams. Caroline Ketcham, Eric Hall, Heather Fitz Gibbon, and Helen Walkington (2018) explored the outcomes of multiple faculty mentors collaborating to support one or more students. While students benefit from working alongside faculty who bring different areas of expertise, colleagues also have the opportunity to observe and learn from each other's approaches to the project and interactions with the shared mentee(s), leading to significant outcomes for faculty development (Ketcham et al., 2017, 2018).

Facilitating Relationships in Work-Integrated Learning and Community-Based Learning

Work-integrated learning and community-based learning projects also are potential sites for relationship-building that could include models of mutual mentoring. Internships, practicums, and other types of work-integrated learning that are completed for university credit often include both a site supervisor and a faculty/staff mentor. While students' relationships with some site supervisors might be bounded by the duration and place of the internship or practicum, these relationships have the potential to develop into enduring mentoring relationships. Likewise, faculty/staff might mentor a student's internship for a semester or develop mentoring relationships that do not end when the student completes the internship. Research by Colleen Nevison, Lauren Cormier, T. Judene Pretti, and David Drewery (2018) on supervisors' satisfaction with co-op students suggests that everyone involved in a work-integrated learning placement—student, site supervisor, and faculty/staff mentor—should attend to relationship-building. They recommend that site supervisors and students collaborate on setting performance expectations and outlining cultural norms for the work site as part of a learning contract and establish regular communication early in the placement to continue working on aligning expectations, in addition to site supervisors and faculty/staff mentors touching base routinely (Nevison et al., 2018). While these types of tasks might seem very instrumental in nature, they provide tools and structures for developing several of the nine factors that Jenny Fleming, Kathryn McLachlan, and T. Judene Pretti (2018) identify as key to developing sustainable work-integrated learning relationships: a focus on learning, shared vision, reciprocity, transparent expectations, appropriate resources, recognition, coordination, reputation protection, and trust. These studies set out to explore supervisor satisfaction and strategies for sustaining relationships between colleges and industry for work-integrated learning, but they highlight the need for intentional relationship-building among all involved with this pedagogy and reinforce that clear communication and transparent goal setting help foster those relationships.

Community-based learning also often creates opportunities for students to develop sustained relationships with community partners and can facilitate encounters with diverse others. In her exploration of a service-learning project as local global learning, 2015–2017 seminar coleader Amanda Sturgill (2020) noted that students were more likely to identify food bank clients "as brave, educated, hardworking, honest, intelligent, and lucky" after interacting with them directly (p. 74). While these interactions during a one-semester course might not have led to longer-term relationships, students' "reflection responses showed a clear shift from an analytical approach to hunger as a problem some people deal with to an empathetic approach where students noted the common humanity they shared with the food bank clients they met" (p. 75). This type of perspective shift certainly is a necessary precursor to establishing a longer-term, reciprocal relationship. Christa S. Bialka and Stacey A. Havlik (2016) studied a service-learning partnership with multiple classes at a university and two high schools and note that the reoccurring interactions among pairs of university and high school students allowed relationships to develop, which in turn made the experience more meaningful for both student groups. Similarly, university students might develop more meaningful relationships with community partners when students have opportunities to participate in community-based learning at the same site over multiple semesters, whether through sequenced experiences in a major or minor curriculum or through a course-based experience followed by a leadership role in a campus service-learning office where students can contribute to maintaining ongoing campus–community partnerships.

In both work-integrated learning and community-based learning contexts, faculty/staff can help students develop relationships with their peers and near peers by facilitating intentional interaction among students. For example, a faculty/staff internship mentor could meet with multiple internship students at the same time, inviting students to share their experiences, help each other process challenges, and make connections to shared coursework. Or an instructor could invite a student who previously participated in a community-based learning partnership to return as an undergraduate teaching assistant in a future semester to share strategies with current students and to facilitate discussion and reflection.

Facilitating Relationships in Residential Learning Communities

Research from the 2017–2019 research seminar on Residential Learning Communities as a High-Impact Practice offers insight on how to foster relationships in these communities. Jennifer Eidum, Lara Lomicka, Warren Chiang, Ghada Endick, and Jill Stratton (2020) studied students' thriving in residential learning communities, using Schreiner's (2016) definition of *thriving* as being "fully engaged intellectually, socially, and emotionally in the college experience" (p. 136). Although residential learning communities often include one or more linked courses, Eidum et al. (2020) did not find a correlation between these courses and thriving. Instead, they write, "Thriving emerges through the engagement of faculty in the overall RLC program, with continued faculty presence," leading the research team to suggest that "promoting informal and formal conversations between faculty and students about major, career, and life questions, as well as faculty involvement in dinners, advising, workshops, and social gatherings" may have a more lasting impact on students' thriving (p. 17). These findings align with research on the importance of social interactions for psychological sense of community, shared earlier in this chapter (Sriram, Weintraub, et al., 2020).

Collectively, the research seminar participants' work points toward the importance of academically and socially supportive climates, two elements in the living-learning communities best practices model (Inkelas et al., 2018), for fostering relationships. Allocating resources to faculty/staff-in-residence programs and designing residential community spaces where faculty/staff can engage informally with students can contribute to relationship-building, and in turn, belonging or thriving.

Facilitating Relationships in On-Campus Student Employment

Staff who supervise student employees also can help students develop meaningful relationships. By scheduling strategic overlap in student work schedules, students can get to know other student employees. Near peers working in the same office often can teach their peer colleagues relevant skills and strategies (e.g., McClellan et al., 2018), facilitating peer-to-peer interactions around authentic tasks.

Of course, on-campus student employment is a key site for relationship-building among students and staff, as well. In chapter 2, I highlighted the Iowa GROW model as a way to acknowledge and build on students' prior knowledge and experiences in student employment. These recurring conversations contribute to relationship-building as supervisors learn more about their student employees' academic lives and professional goals and students see that their supervisors have a vested interest in their current and future success.

Implications and Recommendations for Individual Faculty and Staff

Within the classroom, whether in person or online, instructors can facilitate relationship-building by:

- addressing students by name
- making time (if even briefly) to offer emotional support, not only academic support
- creating opportunities for students to collaborate with peers

Beyond the classroom, faculty and staff can facilitate intentional opportunities for students to extend their networks by working with peers and near peers toward shared goals or connecting with industry and community partners. They also can participate in formal and informal interactions that extend beyond an academic focus to attend to broader life questions.

- How might I facilitate opportunities for peer and near-peer mentoring?
- How might I connect students with alumni and/or community or disciplinary professionals?
- What types of support do I feel comfortable offering students myself, and what types of support would I rather address by helping students build relationships with others?

Implications and Recommendations for Program and Institution Leaders

Relationship-building requires a valuable commodity: time. Therefore, programs and institutions that are striving to create relationship-rich cultures should inventory the structures and systems that support—or act as barriers to—fostering relationships. As Felten and Lambert (2020) write:

> Institutional leaders—trustees, administrators, faculty, and staff—need to address basic questions such as: Do meaningful relationships with students really matter on our campus? How are we rewarding those who mentor, advise, and support students? How can we support and encourage everyone on campus to join in a culture encouraging students to seek meaningful relationships and mentors? (p. 150)

Daily schedules need to accommodate time for meaningful conversations. Campus spaces need to welcome both formal and informal interactions.

And annual review and promotion criteria need to recognize the value of this work.

Facilitating relationships is the second cornerstone for fostering students' active participation in their own lifelong learning. When students have a web of meaningful relationships, certain outcomes are more likely:

- feeling a sense of belonging on campus
- persisting in their college studies
- achieving academic success in their college studies
- considering their college experience rewarding

In addition, having meaningful relationships contributes to using feedback, the focus of the next chapter, and to making connections to broader contexts (chapter 5). Therefore, facilitating relationships should be a faculty/staff and institutional priority for fostering engaged learning.

4

OFFERING FEEDBACK

Sam scanned the lounge area in the student center. Today is the university president's monthly table tennis time, so the lounge is a bit more boisterous as students wait to challenge her in a game. Rounding a corner, Sam spots their first-year seminar teacher and three classmates in a corner nook, laptops open. Joining them, Sam settles into an overstuffed chair and opens their laptop, their peers' drafts already open with electronic comments anchoring Sam's feedback to specific sections. Sam's professor explains that the group will talk about one draft at a time, first describing what they see as readers of the draft, then evaluating how the draft meets—or doesn't meet—the assignment criteria, and finally suggesting specific strategies the writer could try as they revise. Initially Sam is hesitant to share their feedback, but when a classmate makes a similar observation to one Sam noted in their electronic comments, Sam jumps in with a "Me, too," and adds more details about their reaction. When the professor asks Sam to share their "describe" feedback first for the next peer's draft, Sam feels more comfortable weighing in, realizing that everyone in the group is trying to support each other. Sam also didn't miss that their professor correctly used each student's pronouns throughout the group conference, even their own, adding to their comfort level with this small group.

Later in the day, Sam's still thinking about the "describe–evaluate–suggest" feedback strategy while logging into the office computer at their on-campus job. Sam's supervisor left a message on the office messaging system, and Sam laughs as they recognize the now familiar structure:

> Sam, the draft flyer has some fun, eye-catching graphics, and it gives the general details about the event, like date and time. This version covers the basics we talked about, but it's still a little text heavy. Why don't you try using bullet points to simplify the details, and maybe add a QR code for the web page so students can find more information?

Why Offering Feedback Matters

When faculty, staff, and peers offer constructive feedback—both formative and summative—students are better equipped to advance their understanding and application of key concepts. Drawing from both engaged learning and writing studies scholarship, this chapter offers strategies for increasing the number of substantive feedback cycles by incorporating faculty/staff feedback, peer feedback, and self-assessment. Ultimately, the goal is to create a culture of feedback that includes students as self-regulated learners (e.g., Nicol & Macfarlane-Dick, 2006) who understand when and how to ask for feedback and then how to use the feedback they receive. Therefore, creating a culture of feedback relies on the two cornerstone key practices of building on prior knowledge and facilitating relationships (see Figure 4.1).

But why does getting feedback matter? Quite simply, feedback helps us learn, which is why Arthur W. Chickering and Zelda F. Gamson (1987),

Figure 4.1. Giving feedback as a key practice for fostering engaged learning.

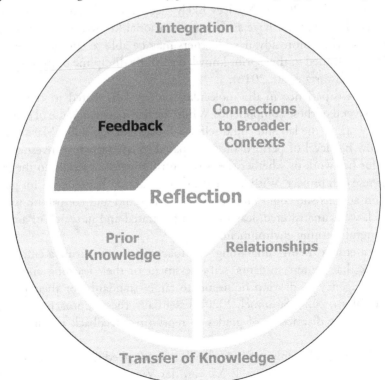

Susan Ambrose et al. (2010), and George Kuh et al. (2017) identify feedback as necessary to support learning. Ambrose et al. (2010), for example, write that "goal-directed *practice coupled with* targeted *feedback are critical to learning*" (p. 125, emphasis in original) and describe a cycle of practice and feedback in which students' observed practice prompts focused feedback, which in turn informs students' additional practice. While it's tempting to associate feedback primarily with grades or performance reviews, formative feedback—feedback given to support student learning, not as a summative assessment—can happen multiple times in a practice and feedback cycle. In his theory of formative assessment, D. Royce Sadler (1989) argues that in order to self-monitor progress, learners need to understand their target goal, compare their abilities or work in relation to the goal, and intentionally strive to move closer to that target goal. Formative feedback can help students compare their current performance level against a standard or goal and assess which actions they can take to advance toward that standard. And ideally, formative feedback includes self-feedback, peer or near-peer feedback, and faculty or staff feedback that students use collectively as self-regulated learners (e.g., Nicol & Macfarlane-Dick, 2006). Novices likely need more feedback from others since they may not have sufficient situational knowledge about target standards, while more advanced learners may be able to engage more self-critique grounded in their prior knowledge of the discipline or professional context (Schwartz et al., 2016).

Maya's experience in the molecular biology lab, shared in chapter 1, lacked several of these components. While she had a general sense of the goal for her work in the lab and could self-assess her basic lab skills, Maya wasn't sure how her level of performance compared to the principal investigator's goals for her work or whether she was contributing successfully to the lab's larger research project. Without a culture of feedback, her requests for guidance on actions she could take to better understand and contribute to the research went unanswered, leaving Maya frustrated and in search of a more meaningful learning environment.

Incidentally, many "ungrading" approaches strive to create a culture of feedback that centers students' self-assessment of their learning and gives students agency to develop or negotiate target standards for their performance (Blum, 2020; Stommel, 2020). Essentially, these approaches attempt to remove the distraction of grades to reprioritize feedback in support of student learning.

With the goal of improving feedback in medical education, Christopher Watling, Erik Driessen, Cees P. M. van der Vleuten, and Lorelei Lingard

(2014) studied the feedback cultures that often develop in competitive sports and music performance. They conclude that the effectiveness of feedback in a learning situation depends on four interrelated conditions:

- clear performance goals
- "specific, timely, actionable and credible" feedback (p. 716)
- learner attention to that feedback as something that could help them improve their performance
- a learning culture that normalizes and facilitates the exchange of feedback

Watling et al. (2014) link this type of feedback-friendly learning culture to a relationship-rich culture: "Across [disciplinary] cultures, meaningful feedback seemed more likely to occur in the context of a strong, trusting relationship between the teacher and learner" (p. 718). Moreover, when feedback came from a trusted teacher who the learner identified as having shared goals for the learner's performance, learners were more likely to embrace even critical feedback as helpful. Watling et al. emphasize, "Learning culture neither creates motivated learners nor defines 'good feedback.' Rather, it creates the conditions in which good feedback can occur, and opportunities for it to do so and for learners to respond" (p. 720). In Sam's interactions with their first-year seminar instructor and peers and with their work supervisor, we see these components in play; faculty and staff with whom Sam is developing meaningful relationships have created conditions in which feedback can occur and conveyed expectations for Sam to use that feedback to revise—whether before submitting an assignment for a grade or before printing a flyer for distribution—so that Sam can meet shared learning or work goals.

In addition to supporting goals in college, feedback also positively impacts performance in the workplace after graduation. Often formative feedback from colleagues and clients helps us understand how well we are addressing our audience and purpose for projects. In the 2019 Center for Engaged Learning/Elon Poll, 16% of recent college graduates reported that their greatest writing challenge is adapting to readers' expectations and needs. Knowing how to ask for and incorporate feedback could help these recent graduates explicitly address this challenge by asking coworkers for feedback on early drafts and clients for feedback on later drafts.

Unfortunately, asking for feedback isn't something that comes naturally to most of us, and how you ask for feedback can make a big difference in the quality of feedback you receive, so learning how to request and process feedback can positively impact student success in and beyond college.

Why Faculty and Staff Offering Feedback Matters

Faculty and staff are well positioned to help students assess their current level of performance against course or disciplinary standards. Faculty and staff already have developed more expert knowledge of the skills required to participate in their discipline's or field's community of practice, while students are newcomers or apprentices (e.g., Lave & Wenger, 1991), learning the community's sociocultural norms. Faculty and staff members' expert perspectives are critical for learning, since students may not yet have enough knowledge and experience to self-identify errors in their work or the ways their practices vary from community norms; feedback from a teacher or supervisor helps learners correct errors more efficiently and reduces the risk that learners will continue to practice errors, potentially reinforcing them (Ambrose et al., 2010). Unfortunately, students and alumni report that this feedback often is underrepresented in, or even absent from, their college experiences.

In the 2019 survey of college graduates, 11.2% of respondents indicated that getting useful feedback on writing is the biggest writing challenge they have encountered since graduating. This challenge likely has roots in graduates' college experiences. Results from the 2019 NSSE Experiences with Writing Module suggest that 20% of seniors at the 71 institutions using the module reported that they had *not* received feedback from a classmate, friend, or family member about a draft before turning in the final assignment—for *any* writing assignment; 24% had received feedback about a draft for only a few writing assignments (NSSE, 2019b). The 2019 Center for Engaged Learning/Elon Poll survey asked recent college graduates about project feedback more broadly—not limited to writing assignments—and reports similar findings:

- 7.1% report never receiving feedback from faculty/staff on any submitted, final projects, during their entire time in college.
- 9.9% report never receiving feedback from faculty/staff to guide their work before submitting a final version.
- 14% report never receiving feedback from peers to guide their work before submitting a final version.
- 24% reported only once receiving feedback from faculty/staff to guide their work before submitting a final version.
- 28% reported only once receiving feedback from peers to guide their work before submitting a final version.

Moreover, college graduates who reported not receiving feedback from one of these groups often don't receive *any* feedback. In the 2019 Elon Poll, 35%

of the college graduates who reported never receiving feedback from faculty/staff to guide their work before submitting a final version also reported never receiving feedback from peers on work-in-progress. Even more startling, 41% of the college graduates who reported never receiving feedback from faculty/staff to guide their work before they submitted a final version also reported never receiving feedback from faculty/staff on a submitted, final project.

Participants in the 2015–2017 research seminar on Integrating Global Learning with the University Experience share an additional perspective on why faculty/staff need to increase feedback opportunities for students. In the *Elon Statement on Global Learning*, they note that "pre-testing and debriefing of student intercultural competency prior to leaving campus" can support learning during study away experiences (Center for Engaged Learning, 2017, para. 15). Offering timely feedback helps students adjust their ongoing practices and make sense of troublesome knowledge when new information or experiences conflict with their prior cultural understandings. For example, research seminar participants Melanie Rathburn, Jodi Malmgren, Ashley Brenner, Michael Carignan, Jane Hardy, and Andrea Paras (2020) used guided reflections to assess students' intercultural competence and observe:

> Written feedback on their reflections . . . likely influenced the quality and depth of reflection. . . . The instructor's questions and comments about students' understanding of an intercultural interaction may have helped them to reconcile encounters and may have provided them with knowledge and support as they sought to understand different perspectives and ways to adapt. (p. 93)

In this example, reflection (the focus of chapter 6) and feedback interweave to foster students' active and intentional participation in their ongoing learning.

Why Students Offering Feedback Matters

When students offer their peers feedback, they have opportunities both to reflect on their own work in relation to their peers' and to practice a critical skill for their future professional roles. Even if students receive predominantly positive feedback from classmates, the act of reviewing others' work helps them assess their own and consider ways to improve it (Hart-Davidson & Graham Meeks, 2020; Mutch et al., 2018). Bill Hart-Davidson and Melissa Graham Meeks (2020) explain that "giver's gain" occurs because "giving helpful feedback is a way to practice something students must do themselves to be successful: revise their own work" (p. 79). Kwangsu Cho and Charles MacArthur (2011) unpack this connection, noting that peer review activities require students to "take the perspective of readers," identify challenges in the draft text, and offer explanations for suggested revisions (p. 75). As Meeks (2017) writes:

> Giver's gain comes from actively thinking alongside another writer:
>
> - What you read, you too can imitate.
> - What you detect, you too can correct.
> - What you explain, you too can retain.
> - What you suggest, you too can try.
>
> It can be as a simple as a reviewer saying, "You are missing this requirement; oh, I think I left it out too!" (para. 1)

When students can identify room for improvement in peers' work and offer concrete suggestions for revision, they likely can turn that same critical eye and understanding of the assignment to their own writing. As a result, Hart-Davidson and Graham Meeks suggest that the number of words given during peer review for a writing assignment is a better predictor of course performance than the number of words students write for their own projects.

Figure 4.2 tracks three of my own students' word counts—the amount of feedback they gave their classmates—across 10 review tasks in a first-year writing course. At the semester midpoint, I shared similar graphs with each student, showing their word count trends in relation to the class average so that I could talk with them about how they might improve the feedback they give their peers—and why doing so might help them improve their own writing. With IRB-approval, I'm sharing three anonymized student examples here, using data pulled from my course's Eli Review peer feedback activities. Instructors could use this type of data for teaching purposes without seeking IRB approval, though. What might "giver's gain" enable me to predict about these three students' performances?

Student A's word count across review tasks typically remains at or below the class average, suggesting that they might not be as confident as other students about their understanding of the assignments or their ability to give helpful feedback. Student B's word count starts lower than average for the first few assignments but increases as the semester progresses, correlating with increased confidence in their understanding of the assignments. In addition, after review task 3, Student B began connecting the review tasks to prior experience as a high school writing center consultant, identifying more with their role as a reviewer and placing more value on the review tasks.

Figure 4.2. Word count by reviewer across 10 review tasks.

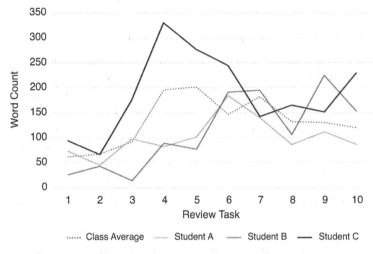

Student C is a consistent giver, frequently exceeding the class average word count; they are confident about their understanding of the assignments and typically follow up with the instructor when they have questions.

Tracking each student's number of words given during peer review gave me another way to assess my students' understanding of the assignments and writing strategies. And looking at the actual content of their peer feedback helped me identify common challenges when I saw several peers offering similar feedback across drafts. As a result, I was able to clarify expectations and revisit specific strategies while students were still revising their drafts and could apply both peer-to-peer and instructor-to-class feedback to their revisions.

Cho and MacArthur (2011) suggest, "Peer reviewing can be practically valuable in producing more in-class writing opportunities because students are rich resources for feedback on peer writing" (p. 73). Peer feedback also can improve students' academic self-concept, or their self-assessment of their abilities in specific academic contexts (Simonsmeier et al., 2020). As Cho and MacArthur (2011) note, "Reviewing is an evaluative problem-solving process of detecting text problems, diagnosing them, and generating solutions to improve the problems" (pp. 74–75). Analyzing peer examples and applying that analysis to the construction of helpful feedback requires students to engage in critical thinking about the assignment.

Faculty sometimes give up on peer review before seeing these benefits, though. Faculty and students might express doubt about the value of peer feedback, particularly if students haven't received instruction in how to give helpful feedback. To improve student buy-in, Meeks (2016) suggests giving students clear rationales for peer learning, talking about the value of peer learning to their future professional lives, and continuing to give faculty feedback at critical moments.

Of course, peer feedback isn't limited to students' (or recent graduates') written projects or to classroom contexts. As I was drafting this chapter, a campus tour group passed my office window, and I heard an experienced student tour guide discreetly giving feedback to a guide-in-training as they transitioned to their next physical talking point. The experienced student guide shared tips about other types of information she integrates into her talking points for that section of campus when her tour group includes visitors with similar interests (e.g., potential majors, religious identities) to their current group. That quick, formative feedback was anchored to the section of campus the group was currently touring (much like a marginal comment can be anchored to a specific section of a paper), so the contextual cues might help the guide-in-training remember to apply the feedback for the next tour passing that spot; yet the just-in-time feedback also likely informed the guide-in-training's discussions with visitors for the rest of the tour.

These opportunities to engage in peer feedback—whether within or beyond the classroom—also help students develop capacities they'll need for lifelong and lifewide learning. In the 2019 Center for Engaged Learning/ Elon Poll survey of recent college graduates, approximately 60% of respondents indicated that giving feedback to others is very important or somewhat important to their day-to-day life. Yet 32.5%—nearly one third of survey respondents—report not developing this skill while in college, which is particularly unfortunate in light of the research illustrating "giver's gain."

Feedback as an Opportunity to Address Inequities

Because receiving and responding to feedback is such a key component of the learning process, attending to *how* we give feedback is critical. Feedback practices can reaffirm systemic inequities, or they can be opportunities to enact social justice. Tracie Marcella Addy, Derek Dube, Khadijah A. Mitchell, and Mallory E. SoRelle (2021) write that inclusive instructors give "constructive feedback throughout their [students'] learning process. This means more than the instructor just assigning a grade, but spending time to help students identify how to improve moving forward through written response and through conversation and modeling" (pp. 107–108). Grading rubrics evolved as an attempt to achieve more consistency in assessment across students' submissions and to pair a summative assessment with criteria that could guide students' future improvement by detailing where their work fell short of expectations. Used uncritically, however, Valerie

Balester (2012) warns that rubrics can oversimplify expectations for writing and place already minoritized students of color and students for whom English is an additional language at greater disadvantage. Balester (2012) advocates embracing the linguistic variety students bring to our courses and reminds us that languages evolve within social-cultural contexts, so some of the conventions faculty and staff learned as students may have changed. Multicultural assessments, then, acknowledge that language is rhetorically situated (i.e., influenced by the context in which it is used, including factors like the intended audience and the purpose for communicating), that the rhetorical situation includes the writer's own identity, and that cocreation with students of assessment tools like rubrics can disrupt power dynamics around language standards within that situation (Balester, 2012; Inoue, 2004).

After unpacking his own parallel concerns with rubrics, Jessie Stommel (2020) suggests that when students construct rubrics, "the making of the rubric becomes an act of learning itself rather than a device (or set of assumptions) created entirely in advance of students arriving to a course" (p. 39). This perspective reiterates that student construction or coconstruction of feedback tools may help faculty and students focus on describing students' progress toward learning goals in relation to their own prior knowledge (an underlying goal of feedback), rather than on measuring students' work against potentially biased markers (see also Bovill, 2020, for more information on cocreation).

Offering Feedback in the Classroom

When I talk with instructors about offering feedback on student work, I often advocate using a combination of marginal comments that can anchor feedback to specific examples and a summary statement that helps students prioritize the feedback in relation to the assignment guidelines. I also recommend limiting the number of marginal comments and keeping them focused on characteristics of the student work that are most relevant to the assignment guidelines and goals. Often, practicing multicultural assessment for writing assignments means opting to mark only repeated deviations from Edited American English, not every sentence-level "mistake," allowing students to consider whether attending to the deviation would help them more successfully appeal to specific audiences. The bulk of marginal comments instead focuses on strong examples in the student's text, sections that might benefit from elaboration (or conciseness), and questions I have as a reader as I'm engaging with the text. Feedback on other types of student work can enact similar prioritization, focusing comments on aspects of the work that meet, or fall short of, the specific goals for the assignment. This prioritization helps students process the feedback that's most relevant to the current learning goals without overwhelming them with well-intentioned but less immediately imperative information (Ambrose et al., 2010). Prioritized feedback also is more likely to use language from the assignment guidelines and associated learning objectives, making it easier for students to "decode" the feedback and apply it to future work (Winstone & Carless, 2020).

Bill Hart-Davidson offers a dynamic strategy for summary comments that also prioritizes feedback in relation to the assignment goals:

- Describe what you as a reader see the text accomplishing.
- Evaluate the text in relation to the assignment criteria.
- Suggest specific ideas for revision (Eli Review, 2016).

This formula can help instructors focus on "specific, timely, actionable and credible" feedback (Watling et al., 2014, p. 716) aligned with the assignment criteria (which hopefully align with the primary goals for the assignment). If the sequencing of activities within the course enables students to act on the feedback, using it to revise the same project or explicitly cuing students to apply it to a future assignment, the "suggest" portion of the describe–evaluate–suggest strategy further contributes to a feedback culture in which students have agency to actively and intentionally engage with the feedback they receive (Winstone & Carless, 2020).

As a professional writing teacher, much of the feedback I give is on written or multimedia texts, but instructors from other disciplines can make parallel distinctions in the types of feedback they give. Focusing on mathematics, for instance, Roar Stovner, Kirsti Klette, and Guri Nortvedt (2021) distinguish among procedural feedback and two types of substantive feedback—conceptual feedback and feedback on mathematical practices. Procedural feedback "focuses on correctly executing steps in a solution procedure" (p. 4) and could entail anchored feedback demonstrating a correction to a recurring mistake with a calculation procedure. Conceptual feedback "focuses on relations between concepts, representations, definitions, theorems, etc." (p. 4) and could entail anchored feedback annotating the component parts of an equation to help clarify how they function independently and collectively. Feedback on mathematical practices "focuses on how the student has engaged in mathematical practices, such as problem-solving, constructing viable arguments, or modeling" (p. 4) and might consist of a summary comment that compliments a student's problem-solving strategy or clarifies how to adapt a strategy for other calculations.

Feedback on mathematical practices could use the describe–evaluate–suggest framework to succinctly describe what the instructor sees a student doing with a problem set, evaluate the effectiveness of those strategies, and suggest alternatives to or extensions of that work.

The describe–evaluate–suggest strategy also works well for peer feedback, giving students specific prompts for considering how peers' drafts respond to the assignment guidelines and suggesting possible revisions.

Integrating Opportunities for Others to Give Feedback

As discussed previously, faculty do not have to be the only source of feedback. Devoting time to peer feedback of written drafts or other assignments, using the describe–evaluate–suggest framework or similar strategies, can lead to stronger revised submissions, particularly in a class with a feedback culture. Telling students about "giver's gain" and acknowledging their potential strengths as reviewers can build students' sense of agency and commitment to the process.

Integrating one-to-one or small-group feedback conferences with students offers an additional strategy for giving timely feedback—while building relationships with students. In Sam's experience, for example, small-group feedback conferences allowed their instructor to model the describe–evaluate–suggest heuristic, and the instructor was present to prompt clarification or follow-up details if students didn't ask for them. The conferences help normalize giving and receiving feedback, contributing to a feedback culture.

Depending on the nature of the project, faculty also could invite clients or community partners to give feedback to the students. Because students may see these audiences as more authentic than the instructor, students often demonstrate a commitment to acting on their feedback.

Criteria Cocreation for Peer and Faculty Feedback

In courses ranging from first-year general education requirements to upper-level undergraduate courses in the major to graduate-level courses, I routinely cocreate assignment criteria with students. As Catherine Bovill (2020) explains, "Whole-class co-creation in learning and teaching involves inviting a whole group of students who are studying together in any teaching setting face-to-face or online, to actively collaborate and negotiate with the teacher and each other, elements of the learning process" (p. 1025).

After introducing the assignment parameters and discussing the audience(s) and purpose(s) for the products students will submit, I ask students to work in groups to brainstorm criteria for a "good" example of the product. Often these discussions are informed by professional or student examples. To move students beyond expectations for style or grammar, I ask students to consider the following:

- What are characteristics of a successful example of the product that achieves its intended purpose?
- What are characteristics of a successful example of the product that is tailored to the audience's expectations?
- What organizational strategies do successful examples use, and why might they be effective?

Based on their analyses, groups propose evaluation criteria and share their criteria with the rest of the class on a whiteboard or in a shared electronic document. We then look for similarities across the groups' suggested criteria and negotiate any differences until we have a cohesive set of criteria. The criteria then become our guiding document for peer-to-peer feedback as students work on drafts and for my evaluation of the final product.

Although codeveloping criteria takes more class time than if I designed the criteria on my own, the analysis activity in small groups and the whole-class discussion give me an opportunity to assess how well students understand the goals of the assignment and to address questions or misconceptions early in the process. As discussed previously, cocreation also enacts a multicultural assessment philosophy (e.g., Balester, 2012; Inoue, 2004) that engages students in discussion of criteria as socially constructed and often specific to the discipline or to the audience and purpose for the product. Bovill (2020) also argues that "whole-class approaches [to cocreation] require, but also enhance, positive relationships between the teacher and a whole group of students, and between the students in a class" (pp. 1029–1030), so while I discuss cocreation here in relation to providing frequent feedback, this strategy also facilitates relationships (see chapter 3).

Peer Educators

Students can take a key role in offering feedback, even if they aren't enrolled in the course. While many peer educator programs are housed in learning or tutoring centers and require students to go to them, some programs embed near peers in the classroom. Initial models, emerging as early as the 1970s, often focused on supplemental instruction, but peer educators also can play key roles during regular class time, facilitating small-group discussions and offering feedback on work-in-progress (Smith, 2008). More recent efforts to facilitate course-based undergraduate research experiences often rely on embedded near peers to offer just-in-time feedback (Sadika et al., 2022). And some medical education programs rely on peer-assisted learning to establish a feedback culture in which near peers can offer timely, constructive feedback with action plans for moving closer to performance goals (Magee et al., 2012).

In addition to supporting other students' learning, peer educators often are well positioned to share feedback with faculty regarding students' frequently asked questions or recurring challenges with course content (Wilson & Arendale, 2011).

Disciplinary Writing Consultants

Disciplinary writing consultants are one example of specialized peer educators. At universities with strong writing across the curriculum and writing center partnerships, tutor-linked courses or course-linked peer tutoring (two of the many names for similar programs) help writing center consultants learn disciplinary expectations for writing so that they are better equipped to offer actionable feedback to students in the linked courses (Mullin, 2001; Soven, 2001). At Elon University, for example, experienced writing center consultants can apply to serve as disciplinary writing consultants. In this role, the consultants meet with the faculty member before new writing projects are introduced, attend some classes, and connect with students via one-to-one conferences, small-group sessions, or in-class activities. The program:

> Helps students . . . learn more about writing in discipline/disciplinary conventions, assists students . . . [with] learn[ing] about their strengths and weaknesses as writers, and helps students learn about the value of peer review and the benefits of visiting a writing consultant. (Elon University Center for Writing Excellence, n.d., para. 2)

In a multi-institutional study of disciplinary or course-embedded writing consultants, near-peer consultants noted that they support their peers in developing help-seeking and collaboration strategies and reinforce a writing process that values seeking and engaging with feedback (Bleakney et al., 2020). Yet the consultants and faculty members often also learn from each other as consultants share students' questions about an assignment or suggest low-stakes writing activities to support larger projects. Heather Robinson and Jonathan Hall (2013) describe a variation on this model that employs graduate students as writing fellows who work with both faculty teaching writing-intensive courses and writing center tutors to create resources focused on aspects of assignments that have been troubling for students.

It Takes a Village—Feedback Integrated Throughout a Degree Program

Faculty in the professional writing and rhetoric major at Elon University build multiple rounds of feedback into the drafting process for a required senior ePortfolio (see Moore et al., 2018). The ePortfolio is introduced in two 200-level courses, allowing students to experiment with ePortfolio design (in a technology studio) and to draft a section of their ePortfolio (in an introductory theory and practice course). Course faculty provide feedback on these early efforts, and students continue to have opportunities to draft sections of their ePortfolios in subsequent courses and as part of the academic component of a required internship. Students also receive feedback from their faculty advisors. At each preregistration advising appointment, students share an artifact from their portfolio and an accompanying reflection. As a result, by their senior year, students have drafted and received feedback on multiple items and organizational sections of their portfolios. Faculty encourage seniors to collaborate in working groups with their peers as they revise their portfolio for external review, and in addition to that peer feedback, students receive a final round of faculty feedback from the program coordinator and a subset of other faculty approximately a month before the "final" portfolio is due. Since an external reviewer also provides students feedback—in individualized letters to each student—seniors often use this additional round of feedback to guide revisions as they prepare for their job search or develop a plan for maintaining their ePortfolio to showcase their professional work even after they graduate.

Video and Other Technology-Enabled Feedback

While the preceding examples focus on written or oral feedback, some teachers are experimenting with video feedback. Giving video-recorded feedback can help instructors convey tone and nonverbal cues, leading students to identify more connections with the instructor and contributing to a "humanized" learning experience (Marshall et al., 2020). Students can use video recordings to facilitate self-assessment of their practice-oriented performance (e.g., lab skills, dance or music performance, patient simulations) and can share videos with instructors, supervisors, or mentors for additional feedback (Cheng, 2018; Epstein et al., 2020). And 2011–2013 research seminar participant Stuart Blythe (2016/2017) has used screen capture with students to document their responses to feedback they receive from internship supervisors (with the end goal of promoting student transfer of learning, the focus of chapter 7).

Other feedback technologies can facilitate nearly immediate feedback, while students are still in the classroom. For example, some online polls and quizzes allow students to enter their responses using their smartphones, computers, or clickers; the software then displays class responses instantly, enabling faculty to show students the range of responses and discuss them. If students' responses are split among several options, faculty can facilitate discussion about the concept, enabling students to share their understanding and to receive immediate feedback. Indeed, a key affordance of classroom polling technologies is the ability to create space for these timely, guided discussions among peers (Winstone & Carless, 2020), contributing to a feedback culture. Some classroom polling systems also summarize for the instructor the questions that most challenged students, which could guide the review of the associated concepts during future class sessions. Of course, the tools alone do not foster engaged learning, but when faculty use these tools to help students assess their performance in relation to clear learning goals, they can help students actively and intentionally participate in their learning.

Offering Feedback Beyond the Classroom

The describe–evaluate–suggest strategy can be equally helpful beyond the classroom, as illustrated in Sam's encounter at their on-campus employment. Although Sam's task was writing-focused, the formula also works with nonwriting tasks, since supervisors, for example, can adapt it to evaluate work-in-progress in relation to contextual expectations for an assigned task.

Offering Feedback in Mentored Undergraduate Research

In mentored undergraduate research (UR), giving timely and actionable feedback helps students improve their technical skills and learn the norms of the discipline; therefore, offering feedback—and helping students learn how to respond to feedback—is an integral part of two salient practices of UR mentors (Shanahan et al., 2015). Yet mentors can share the task of providing feedback to make it more manageable. If mentors build community among a research team and create intentional opportunities for peer and near-peer mentoring, two additional salient practices identified by the 2014–2016 research team, peers and near peers also can offer feedback on research tasks and on presentation and manuscript drafts. Much like some departments or labs host journal clubs to support students' scientific literacy (e.g., Rajhans et al., 2021) and research skills (e.g., Sandefur & Gordy, 2016), research teams could host recurring writing group meetings to create a culture of feedback within the team.

Offering Feedback in Learning Assistance Programs and Writing Centers

Faculty and staff also can encourage students to visit the campus learning assistance center or writing center for additional feedback on project or assignment drafts. Peer tutoring and learning assistance programs create opportunities for students to receive immediate feedback from near peers. Since these types of programs typically rely on students self-electing to participate, they need to continually reimagine how they market their learning and feedback opportunities to students (Arendale, 2010). Fostering a feedback culture across campus can help position learning assistance programs as routine spaces for supplemental feedback.

Requiring visits to learning assistance programs risks overwhelming the center staff and might not lead to students' authentic engagement with the feedback they receive. Many learning assistance centers and writing centers, though, are willing to schedule short consultant/tutor visits to classes to introduce their services and philosophy. And if students have met Maya (introduced in chapter 1) or another peer consultant during a 10-minute class visit, they might feel more comfortable making an appointment with her for consultant feedback on their next assignment.

Many campus writing centers support writers composing texts for an array of contexts. When students know they can visit the writing center for support for class-based writing but also for feedback on job search materials, fellowship applications, and writing for campus or community organizations, the writing center becomes a physical embodiment of a campus's feedback culture.

A study of experienced writing center tutors' strategies documented that tutors often frame their instruction as suggestions and frequently offer explanations for their suggestions with illustrative examples (Mackiewicz & Thompson, 2014). These strategies lead to actionable feedback that might be more timely than instructor feedback. Writing center tutors also receive training to offer credible feedback that is responsive to students' goals (Bleakney et al., 2019), and some writing centers have partnered with faculty across the university on interdisciplinary training to provide meaningful feedback for students in specific disciplines (e.g., Weissbach & Pflueger, 2018, focusing on writing feedback for engineering students).

Offering Feedback in Work-Integrated Learning and Community-Engaged Learning

Workplace supervisors are well positioned to offer students feedback on their progress toward profession-specific competencies. While academic mentors often are most explicitly positioned to offer feedback on students' work-integrated learning, many workplace supervisors want to partner in students' learning (Fleming et al., 2021), and supervisors' feedback can reinforce classroom-based learning (HEQCO, 2016). The Higher Education Quality Council of Ontario suggests that supervisors pair their feedback with setting discrete, achievable goals (HEQCO, 2016), which would help students learn strategies for and practice acting on feedback.

Community-engaged learning affords similar opportunities to engage partners in offering feedback. In a sequenced community-engaged learning opportunity in Notre Dame of Maryland University's pharmacy program, for example, representatives from local agencies (e.g., employment centers, women's centers, etc.) meet with students in their second and third years in the program to inventory students' existing skills and to set goals for developing additional skills; intentional three-way communication among student leaders at each agency, agency representatives, and program faculty further contributes to aligning feedback with these learning goals (Fritsch et al., 2016). At Virginia Tech, a community nutrition course incorporates both formative and summative feedback from service-learning community partners to introduce students to employer expectations before they graduate and to enrich a multifaceted assessment-for-learning plan (Misyak et al., 2016). While offering feedback extends the time community partners invest in students' learning, a study of nonprofit community partners' expectations for service-learning suggests that partners appreciate frequent checkpoints to ensure students' work is mutually beneficial (Rogers & Andrews, 2016). Moreover, feedback from community partners might help students identify the meaningfulness of the work they are doing, contributing to students' sense of purpose (Shin et al., 2018).

If colleges and universities have long-standing partnerships with specific workplaces or community organizations, the institution could offer professional development on giving feedback to student employees or volunteers. While not all partners will want to make time for this type of training, offering continuing education credit or designing the session as a lunch-and-learn community-building event could increase participation. In addition, strategies for offering students feedback likely could be extended or adapted to giving others feedback within the workplace or organization, helping partners enhance their own feedback cultures.

Implications and Recommendations for Individual Faculty and Staff

Faculty and staff can contribute to a feedback culture by offering feedback opportunities:

- peer feedback activities, incorporated into class/work time or scheduled out of class with additional guidance
- introductions to the campus writing center and its consultants
- reader feedback checklists, or questions for readers of the students' choice, that parallel the assignment or project criteria
- coconstruction of assignment or project criteria
- scheduled time for check-ins early in a project cycle when students, student employees, or campus organization leaders are embarking on new-to-them projects

Faculty/staff feedback is critical to fostering students' engaged learning, but for sustainability and to contribute to a campus-wide feedback culture, faculty/staff should ask: Who else can offer my students/employees feedback, and what types of feedback could they provide?

Implications and Recommendations for Program and Institution Leaders

Programs and institutions that value engaged learning strive to cultivate feedback cultures. Curricular mapping, in addition to helping identify potential prior knowledge and experiences students bring to a specific course (as discussed in chapter 2), can be extended to identify where students have opportunities to receive and respond to formative feedback. Program-wide discussions about the types of feedback practices students are encountering across a major or minor can help faculty assess how well their program is enculturating students in disciplinary feedback norms they might encounter postgraduation.

Institutions also can cultivate feedback cultures by offering both faculty and staff professional development on giving timely and actionable feedback. While centers for teaching and learning often facilitate workshops for faculty about grading strategies, hosting professional development on giving feedback and inviting both faculty and staff to attend would allow both groups to see the range of feedback strategies students are encountering across their daily lives—in and beyond the classroom—and might introduce campus community members to additional feedback strategies to try in their specific contexts for working with learners.

Finally, investing in space, staff, and ongoing professional development for campus writing centers and campus learning centers also signals the value of feedback and contributes to a feedback culture.

Ultimately, creating a feedback culture on campus increases the likelihood that students will receive peer, staff, and faculty feedback on work-in-progress so that they can practice responding to feedback. A feedback culture also helps students learn how to ask for timely and actionable feedback so that they are better positioned to request and act on feedback during both their college studies and their postgraduation careers. In other words, practicing asking for and acting on feedback is a key practice for fostering students' active and intentional participation in their lifelong and lifewide learning.

5

FRAMING CONNECTIONS
TO BROADER CONTEXTS

Brooklyn tapped her bus pass against the card reader and made her way to an open seat. It's Tuesday night, so she's headed to the community college for her public speaking class. She'd downloaded the YouTube videos of speeches the professor had assigned the class to watch and played them on her phone while the bus made its way, stop by stop, across town. She was glad she was wearing sunglasses so that the other riders couldn't see her tears as she watched John Boyega's speech at a Black Lives Matter protest; her professor had prompted them to watch for examples of deliberate repetition in the speeches, but she hadn't been prepared for her emotional response to Boyega's call: "We are a physical representation of our support for George Floyd. We are a physical representation in our support for Sandra Bland. We are a physical representation on our support for Trayvon Martin" (Boyega, 2020, 1:38–1:53). She appreciated that class examples and assignments didn't avoid tough topics, but as a woman with a minoritized identity in a predominantly white community, she already felt like she had to have her guard up in class—and on the bus as she made her way to class.

Tuesday and Thursday nights at the community college felt like a homecoming, though. Brooklyn had taken a class there while she was still in high school and then started an associate degree in nursing at the college. During her second semester, her Lifespan Growth and Development class had completed community-based learning projects at several community organizations, and she'd been in a group that organized activities for residents at a nearby assisted living facility. It was a bit challenging to balance the required service hours with her class schedule and work, but she'd appreciated seeing class topics "come to life" during her visits to the facility, and talking to the nurses there had prompted her to transfer to the university across town to enroll in the bachelor of science in nursing program. It sounded like a BSN would open up more job opportunities.

Unfortunately, tuition at the university was more expensive. At the community college, Brooklyn had spent about $5,000 on tuition, fees, books, and supplies for her first year of college. The cost of attendance estimate for the university for fall and spring this year was over $50,000 for tuition, fees, books, and supplies! Thank goodness her parents let her live at home, she knew how to navigate the bus routes, and she'd been able to keep her part-time job. Nevertheless, she still was nervous about having too much debt, so Brooklyn had researched which additional classes might transfer from the community college. Most of her university classes met during the day, so she hoped she could graduate a semester or two earlier if she continued to take courses at the community college a few nights each week. This semester, that meant spending Tuesday and Thursday nights at the college, studying public speaking strategies and giving speeches about the pandemic, racial inequities, and her aspirations for her profession's future.

This chapter offers strategies for scaffolding students' exploration of and practice in real-world applications of their knowledge and skills. These connections to broader contexts can range in scale from carefully selected course content to projects with audiences beyond the instructor to deliberate integration of workplace learning. Moreover, like Brooklyn, many students bring these connections with them to campus as "the prior," gained from the workplace or broader life, so this key practice also provides another opportunity to acknowledge and build on students' prior knowledge and experiences (see Figure 5.1).

Why Framing Connections to Broader Contexts Matters

Since engaged learning entails students actively and intentionally participating in their own learning, not only at discrete moments, but rather as an ongoing, lifelong activity, connections to broader contexts set the stage for that lifelong engaged learning. Framing connections to broader contexts helps students experiment with putting theory into practice, as they navigate complex problems. Typically, connections to broader contexts move students beyond clearly structured problems with known solutions to the more variable problem-solving or teamwork scenarios they'll encounter in the workplace and in their civic lives.

In the 2019 survey of recent college graduates, 61% reported having multiple opportunities to practice real-world applications of what they were learning during college. An additional 27% reported having had one—but

Figure 5.1. Connections to broader contexts as a key practice for fostering engaged learning.

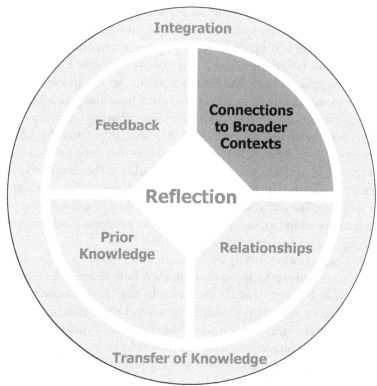

only one—opportunity for that practice. Unfortunately, those numbers drop for students who took classes mostly online, with only 51% of those recent graduates reporting practice with real-world applications. And graduates want more connections between their coursework and broader contexts. Among the U.S. college graduates who answered an open-ended question about how their college could have better prepared them for their job or career, one of the most common responses was that they wanted more practical applications and "real-world" examples. Participants suggested that coursework should be "geared more towards real life scenarios that we could actually apply in the workplace" and desired more experience "relating [course] knowledge to daily tasks in the professional world." These recent graduates called on faculty and staff to "provide more realistic projects and assignments to better prepare me for what I was going to face at work" and wished that in their own coursework they "could have practiced more real-life activities."

Others sought work-integrated learning experiences—internships, field experiences, and practicums—while they had the safety net of college. They called for "more real-life experiences, that is, internships or capstone-type projects" and "more interaction with employees in the field." For some recent graduates, these connections to broader contexts would have facilitated the application of what they were learning while they still could turn to college faculty and staff for support, as the following comments highlight:

> Have me practice the job while under supervision so I could have experience under my belt.

> By getting me out in the real world and helping me experience it firsthand and also giving me opportunities to experience it while still in college.

Studies of workplace supervisor's perspectives on work-integrated learning suggest that supervisors also value offering students "opportunities to make mistakes and learn from these mistakes without serious consequences," particularly when supervisors see themselves as working in partnership with students and college educators to support students' learning (Fleming et al., 2021, p. 716).

For other recent graduates in the 2019 survey, work-integrated learning experiences would have enabled them to gauge their interest in careers and to advance their learning:

> I think putting it in real life situations would have helped get me interested in what I was doing which would have helped me to store that knowledge for the future.

> Have me put my skills to work by having me do an internship, or have me teach the subject matter.

Women are more likely than men to indicate that internships helped them gauge their interest in a profession (NACE, 2021c), but women also are less likely to participate in internships (NACE, 2021b), so they miss out on this potential benefit.

In the 2019 survey, recent graduates also wanted more experience with the types of writing tasks they would encounter in their jobs and more opportunities to get feedback from authentic audiences, such as clients or community partners. They sought "more practical applications. Teach me how to write an email, memo, proposal things like that." Others wished they had opportunities to interact with authentic audiences, as the following comments illustrate:

> I think they could have had us write reports that could be read by other individuals who would be in our careers. A real-world critique of writing would be better than a professor's classroom critique.

> Maybe working for real-life clients.

These alumni comments align with the center's research on preparing students for future writing tasks. As Paula Rosinski (2016/2017), a 2011–2013 research seminar participant and 2019–2021 seminar leader, writes, "Students gain more experience making rhetorical writing decisions based on audience awareness when they are actually writing for real audiences" (p. 259). Client-based projects and community-engaged learning experiences often give students direct contact with their audiences, so they're no longer trying to imagine the wants and needs of a hypothetical audience. Brooklyn, for example, had opportunities to see the unique personalities of each of the assisted living residents with whom she volunteered, and she established a rapport with the facility's nurses. As a result, she was able to make more informed decisions about how to tailor activity materials for them as she completed her community-based learning projects.

As with the other key practices, connections to broader contexts also inform whether recent graduates think going to college was "worth it." Among graduates who never had practice with real-world applications of what they were learning, 41% indicated that, when considering both the costs and benefits of their college experience, going to college was definitely *not* worth it. Therefore, while framing connections to broader contexts should be a campus-wide priority to foster engaged learning, these connections also may improve the perceived value of a college education.

The desires of recent graduates, shared previously, mirror employers' wish lists. An October 2020 survey of executives and hiring managers suggests that employers are "'much more likely to consider' hiring a candidate" who has completed an internship, has experience "working in community settings with people from diverse backgrounds or cultures," or participated in work-study or other employment during college (Finley, 2021, p. 10). The World Economic Forum (2020) predicts that working with people will become increasingly important to employers by 2025, with "analytical thinking and innovation," "active learning and learning strategies," and "complex problem-solving" also topping the list of top skills needed (p. 36). Intentionally facilitating connections to broader contexts during students' education facilitates these sought-after, transferable skills, as students work with—ideally, diverse—others to address authentic, complex problems, while receiving feedback that can guide their adaptation of strategies.

Framing Connections to Broader Contexts in the Classroom

Integrating current examples, as Brooklyn's public speaking instructor did, quickly connects classroom learning to broader contexts. As she watched John Boyega's Black Lives Matter speech, Brooklyn felt a connection to the topic and could see the potential power of a strategy introduced in class (e.g., deliberate repetition). As I've revised this book in the context of a global pandemic and renewed civic action toward racial justice, I've watched colleagues frame connections between:

- statistical modeling and COVID-19 spread
- visual design strategies and CDC resources
- public health strategies and vaccination initiatives
- data analysis and bias
- document design and accessibility
- archival research methods and entrenched racism

Of course, these examples reflect only a few of the meaningful connections instructors have made between their course content and these contemporary issues.

Moreover, given the vast array of "the prior" that students bring to college classrooms, instructors can—and should—invite students to contribute connections between course content and their experiences, too. Like Nadia (chapter 2), approximately 8 million U.S. college students are adult learners (25 or older), with 5 million of those students enrolled part-time (Renn & Reason, 2021). They often have prior or concurrent work experience. Approximately 1.2 million students have military experience (Renn & Reason, 2021). Likely, some aspect of that employment history—or adult learners' other lived experiences—connects to course topics in meaningful ways.

Many of these topical connections, as well as the following pedagogical approaches, engage students with "wicked tendencies" (Veltman et al., 2019, p. 136), slightly tamed versions of wicked problems. In 1973, Horst Rittel and Melvin Webber, professors of design and urban planning, introduced the concept of "wicked" problems to describe challenges in society that do not have discrete, describable solutions; instead, responses to the problems operate on a continuum from better to worse, with no ultimate, one-size-fits-all resolution. The COVID-19 global pandemic and entrenched racial bias and injustice are two contemporary examples of wicked problems; other examples include global warming, food insecurity, and natural hazards. Wicked *tendencies* are "problems of reduced wickedness" that retain the characteristics of uncertainty, complexity, and diverse perspectives common to wicked problems, but often allow students to develop potential actions to respond to the problems (Veltman et al., 2019). Wicked tendencies and wicked problems give students practice working with diverse others, negotiating uncertainty, and navigating disciplinary intersections (McCune et al., 2021). As a result, they address many items in recent graduates' and employers' wish lists for how colleges could better prepare graduates for their future work.

While capstone courses are one logical spot for wicked tendencies (Budwig & Jessen-Marshall, 2018), framing connections to broader contexts within other classrooms also enables educators to consider how they might scaffold experiences across the curriculum to better prepare students to tackle these problems. For example, research skills introduced in one course and case-based projects assigned in another collectively could prepare students to work on community-engaged research in a subsequent course. This intentional scaffolding also addresses the ethical concerns associated with newcomer researchers or emerging professionals practicing strategies for the first time with community partners, particularly when community sites have members with marginalized identities (McGrath et al., 2023). The following subsections explore what connections to broader contexts might look like as they are scaffolded across the curriculum.

Framing Connections to Broader Contexts With Course-Based Undergraduate Research

While mentored undergraduate research (UR) often occurs beyond the classroom, course-based UR experiences (CUREs) offer a way to bring authentic research questions into the classroom. Brad Wuetherick, John Willison, and Jenny Olin Shanahan (2018) note that

> UR as a pedagogical strategy requires that students take responsibility for their learning by undertaking an open-ended project and completing the stages of inquiry from engaging a topic and developing a research question to communicating the results of their work. (p. 186)

These unscripted research projects often allow students to pursue topics related to their personal or professional interests.

Moreover, when sequenced throughout a curriculum, CUREs can help students prepare for wicked tendencies as culminating experiences, as Hannah

Bellwoar's example from a professional writing degree program at a small liberal arts college illustrates:

- In Introduction to Professional Writing, an introduction to qualitative research methods, students use interviews to learn about what people write and how they learn to write at work.
- In Public Health Writing, students complete a Community Engaged Learning project, creating public health posters for the health center on campus. Students research the organization they're writing for and the audience, conducting focus groups with members of the audience. . . .
- In Writing Across Media/Writing for Video Production, students create blogs, podcasts, and videos about their chosen areas of inquiry. Students research their audience and their topic. They read about and engage with multiple ways to disseminate their research to their audience. (Moore et al., 2020, p. 40)

Students in the program conduct independent research as a culminating experience, and the embedded CUREs—introducing qualitative research, practicing qualitative research during a community engaged learning project, and learning how to circulate research to an authentic audience—help students develop the capacities they need for a less structured research project centered around their professional interests. Throughout the sequence, the faculty in this program also help students learn how to give and use feedback (as described in chapter 4) and develop peer and near-peer mentoring relationships that complement faculty teaching and mentoring (a focus of chapter 3). Critically for the focus of this chapter, though, students also have multiple opportunities to connect course topics to broader contexts—to professionals, to community partners, and to engaged audiences.

Framing Connections to Broader Contexts With Cases and Client Projects

Case-based pedagogies give students an opportunity to put theory into practice as they consider how to respond to a specific situation that typically has clear boundaries. While cases often are grounded in real examples, cases may limit the parameters for student response or guide learners toward particular discussion or actions in line with course content. Mathews Nkhoma, Narumon Sriratanaviriyakul, and Huy Le Quang's (2017) description of cases illustrates how the pedagogy can embody wicked tensions:

Using discussion cases, students are presented with stories and are put in the role of decision makers. A case ranges from a simple narrative to more complex, detailed reports of a real-world situation or problem, which is

designed for students to evaluate, conceptualize, discuss, apply and solid-
ify concepts and theories learnt in class (Kunselman and Johnson, 2004).
(p. 38)

Case studies can address complex topics that elicit multiple perspectives,
and they give students opportunities to negotiate uncertainties as they
practice applying course content to a real-world scenario. Studying the
learning outcomes of cases in criminal justice classes, Julie C. Kunselman
and Kathrine A. Johnson (2004) conclude, "The use of cases facilitates the
accumulation of knowledge and allows students to progress from conceptu-
alization to application. Integrating case studies will provide well-rounded
critical thinkers, which, in turn, will result in students becoming better
informed" (p. 92). Similarly, in a study of case-based pedagogy in a teacher
education program, Sarah Gravett, Josef de Beer, Rika Odendaal-Kroon,
and Katherine K. Merseth (2017) note that cases promoted student engagement with course topics, allowed students to consider how they would act
as future teachers even before they moved into student teaching, and enabled students to practice applying educational theory to complex scenarios
while they still had scaffolding and opportunities for feedback. Others have
studied case-based learning outcomes in international relations (e.g., Krain,
2016), health professions (e.g., Thistlethwaite et al., 2012), and many other
disciplines, noting similar benefits associated with cases' connections to
broader contexts.

Client projects, sometimes called student consulting projects or client-
sponsored projects, reflect a slightly more "wicked" way to give students
practice applying course knowledge to real-world problems. Students work
with real businesses or organizations on largely unscripted projects. While
client projects still are bounded by the schedule of an academic term and
might have deadlines imposed by an instructor, they are messier than case
studies. As Christina McCale (2008) describes:

Clients or managers may fail to provide all the information, give conflict-
ing information or provide less direction than an entry-level employee
might prefer. Further, students aren't necessarily seeking the presumed,
right answer as prescribed by an author in a text book; in a real situation,
students are acting on and reacting to information that is being gathered in
bits and pieces. (p. 51)

This wicked tendency begins to expose students to the ambiguity than can
exist day to day a workplace, but with more instructional scaffolding than
students might encounter in an internship or in other work-integrated
learning. Moreover, client-based projects often are designed as collaborative

projects, so students can draw on relationships with their peers as they navigate uncertainties.

Maryam Tofighi (2021) used a quasi-experimental design to study the outcomes of client projects for marketing students. Students who worked with real clients scored higher on exams than students who worked on projects approximating cases, even though their project scores were similar. In interviews, students who worked on client projects reported being motivated to produce strong products for their clients. Based on the qualitative study results, Tofighi (2021) suggests:

> Students in the client-based projects perceived higher levels of intellectual growth and skill development than the students in the non-client-based projects. These findings suggest that students form a deeper understanding of marketing research concepts and theories when applying them to solve real-world business problems. Students highlighted that the client-based project helped them develop useful skills to become more employable. (p. 9)

Amplifying this preparation for work theme, some instructors have collaborated on cross-disciplinary client-based projects to give students experience working with team members from other divisions (e.g., Foster & Yaoyuneyong, 2014). Regardless of whether a client project is a single-discipline project or a cross-disciplinary project, this pedagogy prompts students to apply their prior knowledge to an authentic problem, while developing relationships with clients—and often peers—and engaging with feedback from both clients and instructors. In other words, client projects build on three other key practices while enacting connections to broader contexts.

Framing Connections to Broader Contexts Beyond the Classroom

Students navigate broader contexts daily, so campus and community settings beyond the classroom are rich sites for explicitly framing connections to students' learning and inviting them to apply course content.

Framing Connections to Broader Contexts With Service- or Community-Based Learning

While client projects often focus on wicked tendencies with for-profit businesses, service-learning or community-based learning provides similar experiences as students work with, predominantly, nonprofit community partners. Barbara Jacoby (2015) defines *service-learning* as "experiential education in which students engage in activities that address human and community needs, together with structured opportunities for reflection designed to achieve desired learning outcomes" (pp. 1–2). Reflection (the focus of chapter 6) is a critical component, helping students make meaning of the service (or community) experience (Bringle & Hatcher, 1999).

When done well, service-learning has the potential to:

- increase students' sense of social responsibility (Eyler et al., 2001; Jacoby, 2015)
- facilitate students' application of theory to practice (Eyler et al., 2001; Jacoby, 2015)
- draw students' attention to discrepancies between real-world practices and course content, even as it "bring[s] content to life" (Moore, 2013, p. 562)
- help students identify with diverse others in their local community and reduce stereotypes (Eyler et al., 2001; Moore, 2013; Sturgill, 2020)
- foster students' "skills in communication, leadership, and collaboration that are both civic and workplace skills" (Jacoby, 2015, p. 12), contributing to career development (Eyler et al., 2001)

These outcomes align with framing connections to broader contexts, as students build stronger connections with their communities, practice applying course content to real-world challenges in their communities, and develop skills that they can apply to future personal and professional activities.

Amanda Sturgill (2020), a 2015–2017 research seminar leader, further describes the potential of service-learning as *global* learning, writing:

> But learners don't have to cross geopolitical borders to be global learners, which is good news for students whose degree plans, life factors, or finances preclude international travel. Encountering difference in the classroom and through interactions with diverse people through quality domestic off-campus study can, indeed, produce change toward intercultural competence. (p. 70)

Sturgill reminds readers that service-learning has a rich history of "thinking about the important issues of supported encounters with difference and the ethics of having students learn in off-campus contexts" (p. 71), highlighting two pedagogical design questions that should be front-and-center as instructors design connections to broader contexts. As classroom assignments become more wicked and move into spaces beyond the classroom, they often involve more and more others, increasing the number and types of relationships that students might develop and necessitating attention to ethical design (by instructors) and decision-making (by all involved).

Framing Connection to Broader Contexts in Living-Learning Communities

Living-learning communities (LLCs) have the potential to offer thematically-linked connections to broader contexts. Jonathan Manz, Mark Daniel Ward, and Ellen Gundlach (2023), for instance, share the example of students in an animal science LLC visiting a horse farm to learn about caring for the horses and navigating financial decisions associated with the business. Manz et al. also offer an extended example of a data science LLC that engages students from multiple years in authentic research, with more senior students mentoring newer members of the community. While the LLC draws from a degree area, the LLC activities allow students to integrate knowedge from multiple courses—and presumably other experiences like internships—as they "work with real-life, large data sets in a research computing environment" (Manz et al., 2023, p. 154).

Framing Connections to Broader Contexts via UR

Shannon Davis, Duhita Mahatmya, Pamela Garner, and Rebecca Jones (2015) suggest that mentored UR can be a pathway to interdisciplinary research, with team collaborations prompting mentors and students to make connections across disciplines. Much like cross-disciplinary client projects, interdisciplinary research could create space for students to explicitly connect what they're learning in general education courses or minors to disciplinary content in their majors—or for students to work in partnership with peers in other majors to pool knowledge about wicked problems, fostering relationships (chapter 3) while connecting their higher education studies to broader contexts.

In Davis et al.'s (2015) study of interdisciplinary student–faculty pairs, the represented disciplines often were closely related (e.g., a biology student mentored by a chemistry faculty member, psychology students working with biology faculty), with students seemingly hesitant to venture too far beyond their home discipline. Programmatic and institutional structures potentially contribute to this hesitancy, particularly if UR parameters require students to identify mentors in their degree program. When institutions advance interdisciplinary initiatives to foster students' connections to broader contexts, faculty, staff, and administrators should scan institutional policies and structures for any lingering barriers to cross-program collaborations.

Framing Connections to Broader Contexts via Study Away

Members of a 2015–2017 research seminar team—Iris Berdrow, Rebecca Cruise, Ekaterina Levintova, Sabine Smith, Laura Boudon, Dan Paracka, and Paul M. Worley (2020)—highlight the benefits of facilitating study away to help students frame connections to broader contexts:

> Students who studied abroad exhibit higher levels of global learning-related outcomes compared to their nonparticipating peers. Specifically, study abroad participants consistently report more engagement in discussions with people of different racial, ethnic, religious, political, and socioeconomic backgrounds as well as an enhanced ability to work with others, understand people from diverse backgrounds, and solve complex, real-world problems; they also perceive themselves as more informed and active citizens. (p. 67)

Nationally, participation in study abroad is low. In the 2019 survey of recent graduates, only 19% had studied abroad; Open Doors reported in 2020 that only 16.1% of U.S. bachelor's students studied abroad during their undergraduate program; and in the National Survey of Student Engagement of 2020 seniors, only 14% had studied abroad (NSSE, n.d.). That participation rate drops to 11.0% when considering all U.S. undergraduate students, not only those in four-year programs (Open Doors, 2020). Students are more likely to participate in study abroad when they see concrete benefits to their academic and career goals (Berdrow et al., 2020), so promoting the experience's connections to broader contexts might encourage more students to participate.

Andrea Paras, a 2015–2017 research seminar participant, and her colleague, Lynne Mitchell, note that study away also can create (appropriately) challenging connections to broader contexts:

> *Educators and students should embrace—rather than avoid—uncomfortable encounters with difference.* Predeparture programs often focus on helping students to minimize or avoid culture shock. Our research suggests that instructors should prepare students to engage directly with culturally disorienting situations as long as they provide supportive and helpful strategies for student to make meaning from these challenging experiences, whether the students encounter difference at home or abroad. Effective intercultural learning should involve a balance of discomfort followed by reflection and effective resolution strategies in a supportive environment. (Paras & Mitchell, 2020, p. 105, emphasis in original)

In other words, study abroad does not need to minimize the "wickedness" of navigating differences, but students likely learn more from the experience if they're equipped with appropriate strategies for making meaning of those differences and have opportunities to reflect on them (the focus of the next chapter).

Framing Connections to Broader Contexts via Work-Integrated Learning

Work-integrated learning experiences like internships or co-ops give students an opportunity to practice applying, adapting, or transferring "the prior" to a workplace context while they still have support for their learning. Like other work-integrated learning scholars, Jenny Fleming, Anna Rowe, and Denise Jackson (2021) advocate that colleges and universities should partner with industries to provide learning opportunities with authentic problems. Having opportunities to practice applying knowledge and skills shortly after they are learned increases the likelihood that students will successfully transfer them (Fleming et al., 2021). Many workplace supervisors identify as partners in students' education and want to provide an environment that is

> safe for students to be able to share their own ideas with supervisors and work colleagues and for supervisors to actively seek their input and ideas. . . . Workplace activities need to have some challenges, with opportunities to make mistakes and learn from these mistakes without serious consequences. (Fleming et al., 2021, pp. 715–716)

Work-integrated learning experiences provide authentic workplace settings in which students can make connections between their higher education studies and a career field, but they still retain an emphasis on learning, inclusive of supportive relationships and frequent feedback. Gains associated with these high-impact practices often relate to putting theory or classroom knowledge into practice. The Higher Education Quality Council of Ontario (2016) cautions, for example, that the learning gains associated with work-integrated learning are not a product of the work itself, but rather result from the integration of theory and practice. Furthermore, structured opportunities for reflection (the focus of chapter 6) are essential to achieve that integration.

Interestingly, in the 2019 Center for Engaged Learning/Elon Poll survey, 57% of recent graduates who thought going to college was definitely worth it had completed an internship, one type of work-integrated learning.

Implications and Recommendations for Individual Faculty and Staff

Faculty and staff can frame connections to broader contexts through thoughtful topic selection for assignments and projects, such as the following:

- integrating current events into course readings, discussions, and activities
- inviting students to share relevant examples from their work history and other lived experiences
- partnering with students to address campus and community wicked problems

Faculty also can collaborate with colleagues to consider how they might scaffold ongoing connections to broader contexts throughout course sequences or degree requirements. Could courses, for example, integrate related course-based UR experiences that facilitate progressive skills development or provide increasing levels of wickedness? Or could a curricular sequence introduce cases in a lower-level course, followed by client projects or community-based learning in an upper-level course?

Of course, this deliberate sequencing of progressively more complex, real-world tasks doesn't have to be limited to curricular contexts. Staff who supervise student employees can plan for similar evolutions (and on many campuses, staff supervisors already lead the way on this front). For example, a student who schedules social media posts that other office members write could be tasked with researching strategies for enhancing an office's social media engagement. Subsequently, the student could be given opportunities to both write and schedule posts on assigned topics, using the strategies they've researched. Eventually, they also might be tasked with selecting topics and managing the office's social media more holistically, including responding to comments and direct messages. While this example could be adapted for many campus programs, staff who are familiar with students' prior knowledge and experiences (chapter 2) can frame connections to broader contexts that strategically align with program or office goals. An office of sustainability, for instance, could engage students with relevant research experience in surveying campus and community members about current sustainability initiatives. A landscape manager could challenge student employees who have taken relevant water resources or environmental science courses to design a rain garden. And new student orientation programs routinely involve returning students in the design and implementation of safety programming for new students.

All faculty and staff should ask: How might I scaffold students' exploration and practice of real-world applications of knowledge? How does my program's area of study or work connect to the world's wicked problems? And what prior knowledge do students bring to their work with me that I could help them build on to connect to these broader contexts?

Implications and Recommendations for Program and Institution Leaders

Among graduates in the 2019 survey who indicated college was "probably not" or "definitely not" worth the costs associated with it, over half did not participate in internships or work placement; three quarters did not participate in service-learning or community-engaged learning, capstone projects or experiences, or independent research projects; and over 90% did not study abroad (CEL/Elon Poll, 2019). To foster engaged learning—and make college "worth it"—campuses need to integrate these opportunities to connect to broader contexts—both within and beyond the classroom.

Program and institution leaders need to attend to how institutional structures facilitate or hinder connections to broader contexts. In the 2019 survey of recent graduates, for instance, participants who took classes mostly online were less likely to complete internships or work placement and typically did not participate in service-learning or UR. If these opportunities to practice real-world applications are not embedded in online programs, individual course designs and the holistic design of degree programs need to be extra attentive to fostering connections to students' relevant prior and concurrent "real-world" experiences. Students like Nadia (chapter 2), for example, have rich work experiences and might be pursuing a college degree to advance in their careers. And students like Delsin (chapter 3) have lived experiences of navigating cultural boundaries, even without studying away.

Faculty and staff also need support to learn how to foster connections to broader contexts. Focusing on study away contexts, 2015–2017 research seminar participants Prudence Layne, Sarah Glasco, Joan Gillespie, Dana Gross, and Lisa Jasinski (2020) note,

> The institution must embrace the importance of the faculty role and thus faculty preparation and training, acknowledging that faculty, too, must be able to have ample reflection time and venues to process their own learning and experiences. . . . Institutions should invest in developing mentoring relationships among first-time and more seasoned study away leaders. (p. 144)

This recommendation transfers across pedagogies. Institutions must invest in staff and faculty professional development as part of building sustainable connections to broader contexts in and beyond the classroom.

Framing connections to broader contexts helps students actively test their understanding of theories and procedural knowledge, enhancing engaged learning. Students develop and practice strategies that they will need as they work through wicked tendencies and problems as lifelong learners. Yet connections to broader contexts also illustrate the relevancy of higher education studies, contributing to students' satisfaction with their college experience and positively informing their assessment of the value of their studies. Therefore, while framing these connections may require more time and deliberation than some of the key practices, the benefits are multifaceted.

6

FOSTERING REFLECTION ON LEARNING AND SELF

As soon as he entered the campus coffee shop, Lou spotted his supervisor near the small stage that often hosted poetry slams, music groups, and readings. Lou works part-time in campus rec, and at least once a semester since he'd started 2 years ago, his supervisor has invited him to coffee for a more focused conversation about his job. The first time, he'd been nervous that he'd done something wrong, but they'd simply talked about what he was learning as an operations assistant that might be useful for his career goals. Therefore he wasn't surprised that, as soon as they'd grabbed their coffee and traded updates about their weekend adventures, she asked him, "Now that you've had a few weeks as a team leader for the operations team, what are you learning about communicating effectively with your direct reports that you think will help you when you move to a full-time position?"

When Lou was promoted to the team lead position, he'd learned that his supervisors' questions were part of a college-wide push to support students' reflections about their campus jobs. He'd even learned a couple questions he could ask the peers he supervised to help them think about how their own work experiences related to their class experiences, and vice versa. Asking the questions had helped him get to know his peers better and think about what tasks might be best to assign to each of them to help them develop their interests.

"Well, the GROW questions have helped me think about the types of conversations that I can have with team members to figure out how to make use of everyone's strengths. Sometimes you just have to get work done, but when I asked Sam about what they were learning in their classes, I realized that they have great skills for that social media campaign we'd talked about on what kinds of equipment we have and how to check it out.

And Delsin mentioned that he'd like to do more weight room and equipment orientations because talking with our guests during those facilities introductions helped him practice how to adapt techniques for different abilities—something he's been studying in his strength training course. So I think I'm learning how to talk with team members about how we all can contribute to shared projects."

Reflection functions as a facilitator for many of the other key practices (see Figure 6.1). Guided reflection, for example, can prompt students to consider what prior knowledge and experiences might be relevant to a new situation, as explored in chapter 2. It can foster relationship development, the focus of chapter 3, when students pause to consider who in a team is best prepared to pursue specific tasks, as Lou does with his campus rec peers, or who in their relationship network can support specific types of development. Guided reflection also can help students attend to feedback they've received, assess which feedback to prioritize, and plan adjustments

Figure 6.1. Reflections as a facilitator for other key practices for fostering engaged learning.

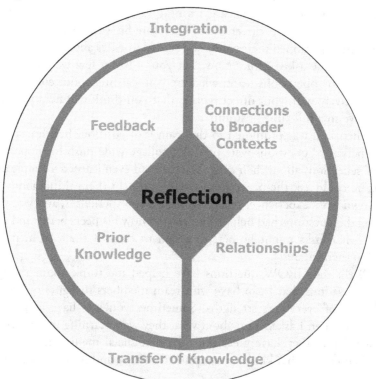

using that feedback, as discussed in chapter 4. And reflection is critical to making sense of how classroom learning connects to broader contexts (chapter 5). Ultimately, opportunities for reflection facilitate integration and transfer of learning (the focus of the next chapter), and opportunities for *metacognitive* reflection prepare students to take more active roles in their own lifelong learning.

Why Fostering Reflection Matters

Broadly, reflection is a process through which humans make sense of experiences. Discussions about reflection often build on the foundational work of John Dewey in *How We Think* (1910) and *Democracy and Education* (1916/2018) and Donald Schön in *The Reflective Practitioner: How Professionals Think in Action* (1983); their collective scholarship contributes to a general awareness of the significant role reflection plays in learning. Writing about reflection in relation to experience, for example, Dewey (1916/2018) suggests, "Thinking is the accurate and deliberate instituting of connections between what is done and its consequences" (p. 161). Experience alone does not lead to learning; humans need to connect the dots between action and reaction, cause and effect, and experiment and outcome. But once we make those connections, our reflection on specific experiences allows us to make sense of corresponding concepts (Schön, 1983). In addition, reflection attends to both affective and cognitive dimensions of experiences (Boud et al., 1985a; Yancey, 1998).

Much like engaged learning entails students actively and intentionally participating in their own learning, this key practice for fostering engaged learning leads to more significant outcomes when students mindfully engage with reflection. Faculty, staff, and peers can prompt reflection by providing guided or directed reflective activities, but "the learner is in total control" (Boud et al., 1985a, p. 11) of the "conscious exploration of one's own experiences" (Silver, 2013, p. 1). David Boud, Rosemary Keogh, and David Walker (1985b) explicitly signal the significance of this connection-making exploration for learning:

> Reflection is an important human activity in which people recapture their experience, think about it, mull it over and evaluate it. It is this working with experience that is important in learning. . . . It is only when we bring our ideas to our consciousness that we can evaluate them and begin to make choices about what we will and will not do. (p. 19)

In other words, the learner must actively engage in making meaning from their experiences. Sometimes that entails reflecting on a specific assignment or activity to consciously identify strengths in performance or areas for improvement. And sometimes that entails reflecting on collective prior experiences to inform future actions.

Moreover, learners can become more skilled at reflection over time. Intentionally engaging students with this key practice in contexts across campus allows them to hone reflective strategies that support their active and intentional integration and transfer of learning. Boud et al. (1985a) caution, though, that educators often make assumptions that learners are engaging in reflection effectively and equitably when individual learners might have different capacities for reflection. In addition, many foundational theories about reflection privilege what happens *during* an experience and *after* the experience (Silver, 2013), downplaying the role of—and learners' meaningful engagement with—prior knowledge and experiences (Yancey, 1998). Fostering reflection, then, depends on acknowledging and building on students' prior knowledge and experiences (the focus of chapter 2), meeting students where they are regarding their capacities for reflection, and helping students develop or refine reflective strategies to put their prior knowledge in dialogue with their goals—which brings us to the concept of metacognition.

Metacognitive reflection allows learners to monitor and regulate their cognitive and affective behavior and to adjust their strategies to achieve their desired goals (Ambrose et al., 2010; National Academies of Sciences, Engineering, and Medicine, 2018). As a result, metacognition is a key practice for taking stock of "the prior" and a necessary precursor to transfer of learning that requires more mindful abstraction of prior knowledge and experiences for application to a new task or context, as the next chapter explores. So, while reflection enables learners to make meaning of discrete experiences, metacognitive reflection functions like a reflection toolkit for *lifelong* learning.

Several participants and teams in the Center for Engaged Learning's research seminars have explored why fostering reflection matters for specific high-impact practices (HIPs) and other meaningful learning experiences. Focusing on writing instruction in college, 2011–2013 research seminar participant Kara Taczak (in Adler Kassner et al., 2016/2017) describes

> reflection as a mode of inquiry [that] encourages both self-monitoring and arousing mindfulness because writers are routinely theorizing about what and how they are learning. Thus, reflection becomes a practice that enables writers to recall, reframe, and relocate their thinking, understanding, and processes about writing and link prior knowledge with new knowledge, as they develop as writers able to transfer knowledge and practices to new situations. (p. 30)

As a result, activities that engage students in metacognitive reflection promote writing transfer, which refers to learners' abilities to adapt prior writing knowledge and experience for new audiences and purposes (Center for Engaged Learning, 2015).

The center's multi-institutional studies also demonstrate the significance of reflection to student learning in study away experiences. Scott Manning, Zachary Frieders, and Lynette Bikos (2020) examined how students' prior experiences inform their global learning in subsequent study abroad. They recommend that faculty who teach study away programs "design reflective work that helps students bridge seemingly unrelated experiences to the challenges of study away. . . . Teaching reflective practice can also help students learn to make connections between the things they believe will help them succeed during study away" (p. 51). Melanie Rathburn, Jodi Malmgren, Ashley Brenner, Michael Carignan, Jane Hardy, and Andrea Paras (2020) used students' written reflections in their study of students' intercultural competence development and quickly identified the power of the reflections themselves

> to understand the nuance of students' intercultural competence development. Students sometimes overestimate their intercultural abilities; as students interact cross-culturally while studying abroad, they may begin to note this tendency. . . . Although IDI [Intercultural Development Inventory] pre/post scores can provide snapshots in time of a student's intercultural competence, the written reflections offer deeper insight. (p. 91)

Like Manning et al. (2020), Rathburn et al. (2020) recommend incorporating reflections into global learning experiences. They suggest that prompts for written reflections

> can be designed to encourage students to reflect on particular elements of the course that are aimed at fostering intercultural competence, such as an individual IDI debrief or class discussion topics. (p. 92)

In addition to enabling students to process specific learning experiences, reflection can facilitate students' integration and transfer of learning. Guided reflections during and after study away help students trace their global learning development, cueing them for more metacognitive awareness of their global learning moving forward (Center for Engaged Learning, 2017).

Similarly, Janet Bean, Chris Beaudoin, Tania von der Heidt, Dave Lewis, and Carol Van Zile-Tamsen, a team from the 2018–2020 research seminar on capstone experiences, conducted a comprehensive review of required capstones in Australia, the United Kingdom, and the United States and noted the central role of reflection in this HIP. Approximately a quarter of the U.S. institutions in their study explicitly invoke reflection in their course descriptions or learning objectives for capstone experiences as a way to facilitate integration of learning or to foster students' agency in their learning (Bean et al., 2023).

Unfortunately, as I shared in the introduction, only 55% of participants in the 2019 Center for Engaged Learning/Elon Poll survey of U.S. college graduates reported having multiple opportunities to reflect on how the different parts of their college experience fit together, and 17% indicated they never had opportunities for that type of reflection. This reflection was even less common for four groups of college graduates:

- 22% of first-generation college graduates reported never having opportunities to reflect on how different parts of their college experience fit together.
- 22% of graduates who earned a two-year degree reported never having these opportunities for reflection.
- 23% of graduates who mostly took classes online did not encounter this reflection.
- 22% of students who commuted (rather than living on campus) reported never reflecting on the integration of their college experiences.

This trend is particularly disheartening given that many college students now experience "unbundled" college curricula as they transfer across multiple institutions during their studies. While it's difficult to discern how many college students have transferred among institutions—and how many times—since different studies set different bars for what counts as transfer, John N. Gardner, Michael J. Rosenberg, and Andrew K. Koch (2021) suggest that "transfer is a primary route to a bachelor's degree in U.S. higher education" (p. 1). By some estimates, 40% of college students begin their postsecondary education at a community college (Fink & Jenkins, 2021), with 80% of those community college students intending to transfer to a four-year institution (Renn & Reason, 2021, citing Jenkins & Fink, 2016). Other students transfer between four-year institutions or begin their college coursework in dual enrollment or early college programs while still enrolled in high school.

Given both these enrollment pathways and a growing perception that degree programs should be "unbundled" to facilitate á la carte enrollment, opportunities for reflection become even more important for helping students "rebundle" and make sense of the component parts of their education (Bass & Enyon, 2016). Randy Bass and Bret Enyon (2016) suggest that "in the emerging digital era, reflection is a crucial lifelong learning skill and an essential process for building integrative and adaptive capacities" (p. 45).

Not only is reflection critical to learning, but opportunities to reflect on how the discrete pieces of a degree program fit together also inform students' perceptions of the value of college. In the 2019 Center for Engaged Learning/Elon Poll survey, 45% of the college graduates who reported that going to college was "definitely *not* worth it" considering both the costs and benefits also reported they had not had opportunities to reflect on how their college experiences were integrated.

Moreover, the lack of practice reflecting for integration may contribute to other challenges. College graduates who reported never having opportunities for this integrative reflection were more likely to also report challenges getting useful feedback on their writing from others, writing in a concise and direct manner, and writing a type of document they had not encountered before (Center for Engaged Learning/Elon Poll, 2019). It's possible that graduates' coursework included instruction and practice in these activities but that students did not have opportunities to reflect on how these core communication skills, often introduced in first-year general education courses, related to their selected disciplinary degree programs.

Fortunately, college graduates were more likely to have had opportunities to reflect on how what they were learning would apply to their futures, with 66% reporting multiple opportunities for that reflection, and 23% reporting one opportunity for forward-looking reflection.

Fostering Reflection in the Classroom

Reflection and metacognition need intentional scaffolding in the curriculum, and students benefit when faculty and staff prompt metacognition at critical moments. As Nancy Chick, Terri Karis, and Cyndi Kernahan (2009) write, "Metacognitive and meta-affective awareness needs to be supported so that students can sort through the complex mix of feelings triggered when new information collides with unexamined prior knowledge" (p. 11). Chick et al. studied metacognitive and meta-affective reflection in race-related courses in literature, psychology, and geography. The reflective activities seemed to support students' learning about race, but the reflections also illustrated that students could get stuck in emotional ruts when new content conflicted with prior knowledge if they didn't have guides and strategies to help them process the troublesome knowledge.

Fostering Reflection in Writing-Intensive Courses

Guided reflection activities have tremendous potential in writing-intensive courses across the curriculum. In first-year writing courses, reflection is a key component of "teaching for transfer" curriculums, in which students not only reflect on their evolving identities as writers but also iteratively reflect on how what they're learning *about* writing shapes their personal theories of writing (Robertson & Taczak, 2017; Yancey et al., 2014). Students might be prompted to reflect on the writing strategies they're learning, as with this prompt: "What rhetorical practices did you find yourself using? Were they effective in the way you presented them?" (Yancey et al., 2014, pp. 165–166). Later, they might engage in forward-looking reflection, as with this prompt: "How might your theory of writing be applied to other writing situations both inside and outside the classroom?" (p. 167).

Similarly, Ashley Hall, Jane Danielewicz, and Jennifer Ware (2013) share a series of reflective prompts that can guide students' developing understanding of how their audience and purpose for specific writing tasks are interrelated, including questions such as, "Based on your most recent discoveries about your audience, are there any revisions you can make to your purpose or goals that will help you meet the expectations of your readers" (p. 162). Like many of the teaching for transfer questions, this type of reflection prompt encourages students to pause and consider what they are learning and how they might apply that new knowledge.

Writing instructors also can scaffold reflection and metacognition with additional questions:

- What steps did you take to learn more about your audience? How might you adapt those audience analysis strategies for future writing assignments?
- What did you already know about writing in this genre (or type of text), and how did you approach learning more about the genre? If you're asked to write an unfamiliar genre in the future, what would you do to learn more about the genre conventions?
- What was challenging about this task? How did you navigate that challenge?
- What did you learn about writing for this audience or purpose that might be applicable to future writing in this course, the field, or another specific anticipated writing context?

Faculty across the university can extend this reflective practice when they introduce writing assignments in their courses. Linda Bergmann and Janet

Zepernick (2007), exploring why students assume their first-year writing knowledge will not transfer to writing in the disciplines, reported, "The attitudes expressed by our respondents suggest that the primary obstacle to such transfer is not that students are *unable* to recognize situations outside FYC [first-year composition] in which those skills can be used, but that students *do not look for* situations because they believe that skills learned in FYC have no value in any other setting" (p. 139, emphasis in original). If faculty ask students, "What did you learn in first-year writing that will help you with this assignment," however, they can prompt learners to reflect on what prior knowledge might be relevant to their new writing task—and signal an expectation that students do, in fact, have prior knowledge that's relevant.

Faculty also can prompt students to engage in forward-looking reflection by asking questions like the following:

- What did you learn or practice by completing this assignment that might be applicable to your future coursework, service-learning, internship, or career?
- How might you adapt your writing if you had a chance to revise this project for a different audience and purpose (e.g., as an example of your capabilities, shared during a hiring process; as an introduction to the topic for readers of a newspaper or popular magazine; as an entry in Wikipedia)?

This type of guided reflection helps students learn reflection "as both a process and product: as before-the-fact activity, during-the-fact activity, and after-the-fact activity, as well as a way to access both cognition and metacognition" (Taczak, in Adler Kassner et al., 2016/2017, p. 29). In other words, this repeated exposure to reflection as students engage with writing assignments across the university helps learners develop their metacognitive reflection toolkit for assessing their relevant prior knowledge for their lifelong and lifewide writing.

Fostering Reflection With Collaborative Projects and Assignments

Although collaborative assignments and projects are officially designated HIPs (Kuh, 2008), questions remain about whether all students in collaborative projects encounter characteristics of HIPs done well, including performance expectations set at appropriately high levels and a significant investment of concentrated effort over time (Buck, 2020b). Furthermore, group projects are ubiquitous in education, but faculty and staff should not assume that students have learned strategies for working effectively in groups (Buck, 2020a).

Guided reflection can enhance the outcomes associated with collaborative assignments. Early in the project, faculty can ask groups to reflect on the prior knowledge and experiences each group member brings to the task at hand, using reflection to acknowledge and build on the prior. Similarly, reflection prompts could guide group members to consider their positive and negative experiences with past collaborative projects so that the group can establish shared expectations for the current assignment as they facilitate relationships within the group. Scrum sessions, like those described in chapter 3, promote reflection on how team members are meeting expectations—both the team's expectations for collaborative activities and the criteria for the assignment; Scrum sessions also create space for giving feedback on work in progress and collectively reflecting on that feedback.

Fostering Reflection in Capstone Courses

As noted earlier, reflection is an explicit outcome for many capstone courses (Bean et al., 2023). What does reflection look like in this context, though? Sometimes it entails prompting students to make connections among prior coursework and senior year experiences that could include service-learning, independent research, or work placements (Kirkscey et al., 2023).

Alternatively, reflection on prior knowledge and experiences can inform forward-looking reflection on what skills or experiences students still need to pursue to work toward future goals. In a senior seminar with an independent capstone project, I ask students to complete an inventory of their skills and to indicate which skills are well honed, which they have but would like to improve, and which skills they do not currently have but would like to develop. The activity is adapted from Susan Maltz and Barbara Grahn's (2003) "Up the Mountain" skill profile. This brief reflective activity prepares students to propose a capstone project that might strengthen an already strong skill area or develop a new one.

In other contexts, ePortfolios function as a culminating or capstone project to facilitate reflection.

Fostering Reflection via ePortfolios

Kathleen Blake Yancey (2017), a 2011–2013 research seminar participant, suggests, "Reflection—a process by which we make our own knowledge—is also at the center of portfolio practice, regardless of medium" (p. 43). In their catalyst framework for ePortfolio, Bret Eynon and Laura Gambino (2018) agree, noting that by "making learning visible, ePortfolio practice done well supports reflection, integration, and deep learning" (p. xxi). In *Catalyst in Action*, they share several case studies that illustrate how to support students' reflections. In Arizona State University's Writers' Studio program, for example, students draw examples from their writing assignments to serve as evidence for their reflections about their learning (Stuckey et al., 2018).

At Elon University, my colleagues and I ask our professional writing and rhetoric seniors to compose a portfolio that showcases "8 to 12 carefully curated artifacts that represent each student's development in the program and his or her identity as a professional writer with a rhetorical world-view" and includes

> contextual reflections for each piece that explain (a) the context for which the artifact was developed, (b) the important rhetorical decisions made in crafting each piece, and (c) a brief summative reflection to explore how the process contributed to the development of . . . his or her professional identity. (Moore et al., 2018, p. 174)

Students ultimately reflect both on how their past projects have contributed to their knowledge development and on what they are prepared to do in their future professional careers.

At LaGuardia Community College, STEM-focused first-year seminar ePortfolios help students make connections across their classes. As Preethi Radhakrishnan, Tonya Hendrix, Kevin Mark, Benjamin Taylor, and Ingrid Veras (2018) write, "Reflection reinforces inquiry skills by following a . . . structured process, asking students to inquire about their own learning experiences, examine evidence of their learning, consider implications, and develop plans for improvement" (p. 225). Like the Elon students, LaGuardia STEM students reflect on their developing identities and career planning.

At the University at Buffalo, students create an ePortfolio after completing their general education coursework, prompting them to reflect on their learning in and across their courses (UB Curriculum, n.d.). A 2018–2020 Center for Engaged Learning research team that studied this ePortfolio requirement as a capstone experience noted that the ePortfolio was "the first time that most of these [University at Buffalo] students have been asked to engage in explicit reflection and to create meaningful connections among past courses, [so] the instructor's role as mentor is essential for success" (Van Zile-Tamsen et al., 2023, p. 79). Across these ePortfolio examples, carefully constructed guidelines help foster reflection, but faculty and staff also play a pivotal role in prompting students' meaning-making as learners select, curate, and reflect on their prior work.

Catalyst in Action includes a range of additional examples of ePortfolio projects that foster reflection across a range of disciplines and institution types. While several of these ePortfolio assignments begin in a specific class, ePortfolios also can extend beyond individual courses to facilitate integrative learning, as I discuss in the next chapter and as highlighted by the preceding Elon, LaGuardia, and University at Buffalo examples.

Fostering Reflection Beyond the Classroom

Ambrose et al. (2010) recommend modeling metacognitive processes and scaffolding students' metacognitive development over time. While their examples are course-based, these holistic strategies are adaptable to contexts beyond the classroom.

Fostering Reflection in On-Campus Employment

In on-campus employment, for instance, supervisors can describe how they would work through a project. When a new student employee first begins assisting with the Center for Engaged Learning's social media, for example, I'll often talk through my own process for scheduling posts:

> We post five days a week, and I like to feature a variety of our resources, so I'll often ask myself, "What types of resources have we posted recently, and what haven't we featured for a while?" If I realize we've been sharing a lot of blog posts, I might pick a video to feature. Or if we haven't featured our books for a while, I'll select one of those to highlight. . . . Which type of resource do you think we should feature next?

Thinking aloud about my process helps model the choices I'm making that typically wouldn't be visible to the student employee. Asking questions of the student invites her to share her thinking and gives me an opportunity to offer feedback on her plan for this recurring task. Of course, other members of our office team also can provide this modeling. Sarah Hansen (2019) notes that "advanced peers can serve as cognitive role models in helping student employees learn how to solve problems and improve performance" (p. 65), as Lou likely does with the peers he leads.

Programs like Iowa GROW, previously mentioned in the discussion of "the prior" (chapter 2), also provide opportunities for scaffolding metacognitive reflection in student employment. As a reminder:

> IOWA GROW® (Guided Reflection on Work) is a brief, structured reflection intervention based on conversations between student employees and their supervisors, and centered around transfer of learning between work and academics. GROW conversations use four basic questions:

- How is your job fitting with your academics?
- What are you learning here at work that you can apply in your classes?
- What are you learning in class that you can apply here at work?
- What are you learning at work that you think you can apply in your future career? (Hansen, 2019, pp. 67–68)

Used iteratively, as Lou experienced, the questions enable students to reflect on their own professional development within their on-campus employment, as well as reflect for integration among their course-based and work-based experiences. Supervisors also can support students' reflection on their holistic identities, particularly as those identities intersect with students' evolving career goals (McClellan et al., 2018)

Fostering Reflection in Work-Integrated Learning

Work-integrated learning, an umbrella classification for pedagogical practices like internships, practicums, field work, and even service- or community-based learning, typically uses reflection-on-action (Schön, 1983) to help students make meaning from experiential learning. For example, Pam Kiser (1998) describes a six-step integrative processing model in which students:

1. Gather data from their work-integrated learning experience.
2. Identify relevant knowledge—from their prior coursework and from an additional review of scholarship.
3. Assess their own reaction to the experience.
4. Explore any dissonance between the relevant disciplinary scholarship and their own perspective on the experience.
5. Describe what they are learning.
6. Develop an action plan for next steps.

Kiser developed this reflection framework for human service students engaged in field placements or practicums, but she and others have adapted it for internships (e.g., Kiser, 2014) and service-learning (e.g., Ash & Clayton, 2004). In Sarah Ash and Patti Clayton's (2004, 2009) "DEAL Model for Critical Reflection," students describe their service-learning experience; analyze or examine the experience in relation to personal, civic, or academic learning objectives; and articulate what they've learned and how that learning can inform future action.

The Higher Education Quality Council of Ontario (2016) operational-izes the DEAL model for application to work-integrated learning with reflection questions such as the following:

Describe:

- What took place?
- Who was and was not present?
- What did you and others do/not do?

Evaluate:

- In what ways did you succeed or do well?
- How has your perspective/thought changed in light of your experience?

Articulate Learning:

- What did you learn?
- How did you learn it?
- Why does it matter? (p. 70, excerpt)

Collectively, these types of question sets prompt students to reflect on *what* they are learning in discrete moments and foster metacognitive reflection about *how* they're learning and *why that learning matters* for their futures.

Across work-integrated learning experiences, faculty and staff can use a variety of reflection tasks, selected based on which activities best align with the experience, context, and learning objectives. Reflection assignments can take the form of surveys, structured dialogue, written assignments (e.g., journaling, essays, case studies), and multimedia texts (HEQCO, 2016). Furthermore, faculty and staff can integrate reflection activities before, during, and after the learning experience and can enlist students' peers and community or workplace partners to facilitate some of these guided reflections (HEQCO, 2016), tapping into and deepening students' relationship networks.

Inspired by Iowa GROW and the HEQCO reflection tools, the Experiential Education Advisory Committee at Elon University partnered with the Center for Engaged Learning to develop the Facilitating Integration and Reflection of the Elon Experiences (FIRE[2]) Toolkit. The FIRE[2] Toolkit includes pre-, during-, and postexperience reflection questions specific to each Elon Experience—global engagement, internships, leadership, service-learning, and undergraduate research. An additional set of cross-cutting questions guides students' selection of Elon Experiences to pursue during their studies, as well as their examination of how the Elon Experiences integrate with the rest of their college education. Faculty and staff can use the questions in advising and mentoring conversations with students, and peer educators have incorporated them into workshops for first-year students. Additional information about the FIRE[2] Toolkit is included in the supplemental resources on the book website.

Fostering Reflection in Study Away

As the center's 2015–2017 research teams established, assigning written reflections before, during, and after study away experiences can help students critically reflect on their intercultural competence. Rathburn et al. (2020) share the following series of prompts (excerpted from supplemental resources available on the center's *Mind the Gap: Global Learning at Home and Abroad* book website):

Time 1 (first day of class):

- What is your cultural background or identity and how does it shape who you are?
- How do you interact effectively with people who are different?

Time 2 (last day prior to departure for study abroad):

- Think about the cultural activities that we have done in class. What is your cultural background or identity and how does it shape who you are?
- How do you interact effectively with people who are different?

Time 3 (last day of study abroad program):

- How did your cultural background or identity shape your experience abroad?
- Think of an intercultural interaction that you experienced or observed while you were abroad. What happened and how did you feel about it?

Time 4 (postreturn, following any postreturn coursework or ~4 weeks after return):

- What cultural skills or insights did you gain in this program/course?
- How did the cultural activities from the predeparture course shape your experience abroad? ("*Mind the Gap* Book Resources," chapter 6 writing prompts download)

Repeated written reflections helped the research team assess students' global learning, but the reflections also "are themselves a cultural intervention; they offer students the opportunity to reflect, potentially moving them further on their intercultural growth trajectory" (Rathburn et al., 2020, p. 93). And because the reflections are written, students can compare their responses over time to see how their intercultural competence has evolved.

Implications and Recommendations for Individual Faculty and Staff

Reflection facilitates meaning-making, helping students identify connections among the prior and new knowledge and experiences. As a result, students benefit from multiple opportunities to reflect—whether in the classroom or beyond. To foster these opportunities, faculty and staff can engage in their own reflection:

- When might I build in opportunities for students' reflection on their learning?
- When I introduce a project or assignment, what prior knowledge do I anticipate students will use to complete the task? Could I use a brief conversation, exit write, or other guiding prompt to invite students to reflect on their relevant prior knowledge?
- When students finish a task, how might I encourage them to think about how the task relates to their future goals?
- Are there natural points during the semester or term when I could ask students about the connections they see among their courses?
- How might I model my own metacognitive processes for students?

Implications and Recommendations for Program and Institution Leaders

Program and institution leaders need to consider how campus structures and policies impact the likelihood that students will encounter opportunities for reflection and to support faculty and staff in developing iterative opportunities for reflection across the curriculum and cocurriculum. Recent U.S. college graduates in the 2019 survey were less likely to encounter opportunities for reflection if they took classes mostly online or commuted to campus. They also were less likely to report opportunities for reflection if they earned a two-year degree. Yet ePortfolio examples from LaGuardia and other community colleges demonstrate that an institutional commit-ment to fostering reflection could build on the affordances of online plat-forms if done well—that is, systematically within and across programs with sufficient professional development and resource support. Regardless of institution type and medium of instruction, program leaders should guide curricular mapping to identify where students already encounter oppor-tunities for reflection and where such opportunities could be added. All students, regardless of how their courses are bundled in their curricular pathways, need recurring prompts for reflection and metacognition to sup-port both their learning at discrete moments and their lifelong learning across and beyond their college educations.

Embedding iterative reflection into students' recurring campus experi-ences and ongoing relationships—in advising conversations and on-campus work, for example—offers a relatively low-resource way to increase stu-dents' opportunities to reflect for both integration and transfer of learning. Nevertheless, staff fostering reflection in these cocurricular spaces also benefit from timely professional development, and recurring assessment of reflection initiatives can help them evolve as campus cultures and traditions shift.

Ideally, reflection becomes part of a campus culture, embedded through-out curricular programs and co- and extracurricular experiences. Reflection facilitates the other key practices, so investing in a culture of reflection will lead to gains in building on the prior, facilitating relationships, offering feedback, and framing connections to broader contexts. In essence, foster-ing reflection binds the key practices and provides the necessary scaffolding for promoting integration and transfer of knowledge, as I explore in the next chapter.

7

PROMOTING INTEGRATION
AND TRANSFER OF
KNOWLEDGE AND SKILLS

Marcus looks at the clock, slightly anxious that so many seats are empty with less than a minute remaining before class begins. He's still not used to the cavalier approach some of his classmates take to class start times and assignment deadlines. In the army, habitual tardiness would lead to verbal counseling, a written reprimand, or even more substantial corrective actions. Unfortunately, the university doesn't give his faculty as much authority as his sergeants had.

After 10 weeks of basic and 14 weeks of advanced individual training, Marcus had spent the rest of his 4 years of active service as a water treatment specialist. Now that he was in a reserve unit, he was using Post-9/11 GI Bill support to work toward a degree in environmental science. He'd enjoyed his job in the army and deliberately sought a degree program that would help him advance in a related civilian career. Marcus hadn't expected so many of his degree requirements to fall seemingly outside that goal; for example, this class—an interdisciplinary capstone seminar—focused on the Winter Olympics. Each section of the required seminar course seemed to have different goals, and none of the sections offered this semester related to environmental science, so he'd selected this section because it was scheduled at a time he could attend and he'd been stationed at U.S. Army Garrison Daegu during the 2018 Olympics in South Korea. While Korea hadn't come up much, he'd been pleasantly surprised when he'd been able to share his experiences with supplying safe water for pop-up communities. He still wasn't sure what the course was supposed to "cap," and sometimes he wondered if he'd overlooked a prereq in sports management or exercise science or ethics. . . . But he'd show up and get it done.

Figure 7.1. Integration and transfer of knowledge as a goal of engaged learning.

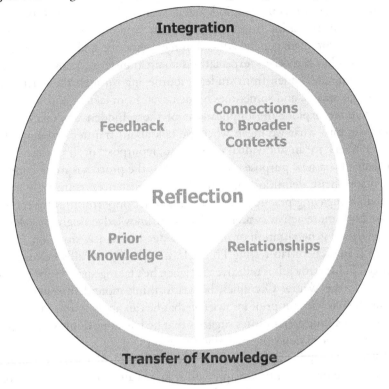

Drawing from studies of integration and transfer of learning, this chapter illustrates how the other six key practices collectively facilitate students' connection-making among new knowledge, prior knowledge, concurrently gained knowledge from other contexts, and future goals (see Figure 7.1).

Why Promoting Integration and Transfer Matters

Higher education curricula are built on the assumption that students will transfer knowledge from course to course—and with the hope that they will integrate what they learn to make meaning from the discrete pieces offered by each individual course. When courses have prerequisites, that expectation of transfer is explicit: This course requires you to have prior knowledge that you will engage, pick up, extend, apply, or perhaps complicate in this (next) class. Even our course numbers often signal a sequencing of sorts; in a 300-level course, faculty anticipate that students will enter with more prior knowledge than in a 200-level course, and perhaps with differently developed dispositions or habits of mind. Yet, as faculty plan individual courses—and as students transition from course to course (and often from discipline to discipline to complete general education requirements) and among courses, work, and other activities—expectations about transfer of knowledge often become implicit, hidden from students journeying through the curriculum and campus spaces, and sometimes hidden even from faculty and staff.

Before we explore the implications of those hidden expectations, we should dig into what we mean when we talk about transfer of knowledge. *Transfer* refers to an individual's ability to repurpose or transform prior knowledge for a new purpose and context, but the process is more complex than that concise definition suggests. In some instances, transfer is nearly automatic, engaging practiced habits, while other opportunities for transfer require both more active awareness that prior knowledge might be relevant and deliberate generalization of that knowledge to the new situation. When Marcus is in a chem lab testing Ph levels, his transfer of skills he routinely practiced in his army job is reflexive. Yet when he's taking an interdisciplinary seminar on the Winter Olympics, he has to think more deliberately about whether he has relevant prior knowledge that he can apply to the course, and his question about prerequisites suggests that he has some doubts about how much of his prior knowledge actually is relevant.

Of course, opportunities for transfer aren't limited to the classroom. Students have opportunities to apply prior knowledge to achieve their goals anytime they engage in a task that's new to them. When Maya uses strategies she developed in her first-year writing class to analyze the audience for a mailing she is creating for her on-campus job, she's engaging in transfer. When Sam applies social media strategies they learned in a marketing class to promote their student organization's next event, they're engaging in transfer. And when Delsin realizes that the reaction he's studying in his organic chemistry lab helps him troubleshoot poor soil conditions in his *gagu's* (grandma's) garden, he's engaging in transfer. Of course transfer also extends to life beyond college; 70% of recent college graduates in the 2019 survey reported that applying existing skills to a new problem was very important to their day-to-day life (CEL/Elon Poll, 2019).

David N. Perkins and Gavriel Salomon offered early—and often cited—ways to describe these different types of transfer. For example, Perkins and Salomon (1992) write that "near transfer occurs when knowledge or skill is used in situations very like the initial context of learning" while "far transfer occurs when people make connections to contexts that intuitively seem vastly different from the context of learning" (p. 202; see also Salomon & Perkins, 1989). When Maya recognizes a calculus problem on her exam is very similar to a homework problem discussed in class, she engages in near transfer to apply the knowledge she practiced while completing the homework problem to the exam question. On the other hand, when Maya realizes that the same calculus technique would have enabled her to determine growth rate of the bacterial culture she studied in the molecular biology lab, she engages in far transfer.

Focusing on the mechanisms that facilitate transfer of learning even when the contexts "seem vastly different," Perkins and Salomon introduced a "low road" transfer model to describe similarities between a new context and prior situations triggering extensively practiced, or nearly automatic, skills. In contrast, "high road" transfer requires deliberate, mindful abstraction of principles to apply them in new situations (Perkins & Salomon, 1988, 1992; Salomon & Perkins, 1989).

King Beach (2003) uses transition and *consequential* transition to make a similar differentiation among types of transfer, describing transition as "the concept we use to understand how knowledge is generalized, or propagated, across social space and time. A transition is consequential when it is consciously reflected on, struggled with, and shifts the individual's sense of self or social position" (p. 42). Far transfer and high road transfer have the potential, then, to reflect consequential transitions if a learner's mindful abstraction not only allows them to apply prior knowledge to a "vastly different" context but also shifts their sense of self.

Colleges and universities' general education requirements often implicitly seek to facilitate these types of consequential transitions, creating a loose structure in which students move among different disciplinary contexts, with faculty hoping that the act of *boundary-crossing* will foster identity shifts toward globally engaged, socially responsible citizens. Drawing from activity systems theory, Terttu Tuomi-Gröhn, Yrjo Engeström, and Michael Young (2003) summarize the concept of boundary-crossing, pointing to an intersection between the learner and context that "involves encountering difference, entering into territory in which we are unfamiliar and, to some significant extent therefore, unqualified" (p. 4). In colleges, each discipline, major, or minor is a unique activity system with its own sense of community, community standards, and tools, and our students often move among many activity systems each day as they navigate both general education courses and courses for their majors. Students also journey among activity systems as they participate in student organizations, student leadership roles, and on- or off-campus employment. Pirjo Lambert (2003) suggests that boundary-crossers employ *boundary objects*, tools that develop at the intersection of these communities or activity systems, to facilitate interaction between and across systems.

Ironically, students likely act as boundary-crossers much more frequently than faculty and staff. Maya, for instance, continues to take calculus classes even after she changes her major to English, including a calculus-based statistics class for her psychology minor. During her senior year, she takes advanced courses in both English and psychology, wraps up an undergraduate research (UR) project in English, works in the writing center and the library's advancement office, and volunteers as a service cochair for a student organization. While she has developed meaningful relationships in each of these activity systems, her faculty, staff supervisors, and mentors rarely cross these varied boundaries.

Although they've evolved primarily as two discrete lines of scholarship, integration of learning relies on transfer. James Barber (2020) writes that "to integrate learning is to connect, apply, and synthesize knowledge and skills across contexts" (p. 1). In other words, integration depends on students being boundary-crossers, transferring prior knowledge from multiple contexts and making connections to achieve a new end goal. William Sullivan (2016) suggests that integrated learning opportunities foster an "intentional weaving" of students' "two main areas of their academic learning: the liberal arts and professional study" and enable students "to demonstrate their ability to put their general knowledge and specific skills to work in providing a public benefit" (p. 31), adding a civic dimension to integration goals. And participants in the 2015–2017 research seminar on global learning note that intentional, recurring, and increasingly complex opportunities for integration of students' off-campus experiences with the rest of their college education "can develop student self-awareness and foster change" (Center for Engaged Learning, 2017, para. 10).

Moreover, like transfer, the ability to integrate learning has value for college graduates. In a survey of employers, 93% indicated that the "ability to integrate ideas/information across settings and contexts" was very important or somewhat important (Finley, 2021, p. 6). Barber (2020) suggests, "In an era when the relevance of a college degree is debated in U.S. society, and the cost of financing higher education is increasingly shifting to individual students and families, integration of learning is a coveted skill that enables students to put the knowledge and skills gained in the college experience to immediate use in other contexts" (p. 10). And as the 2019 survey of college graduates highlights, when students do *not* have multiple opportunities to reflect on how the different parts of their college experience fit together—in other words, how their courses and other college activities integrate—they are more likely to say going to college was definitely *not* worth it.

Randy Bass (2012) cautions, though, "we have reached the end of the era of assuming that the formal curriculum—composed of *bounded, self-contained courses*—is the *primary* place where the most significant learning takes place" (p. 24, emphasis in the original). Students need to encounter *multiple* opportunities to transfer and integrate their learning, in and beyond the classroom. Bass continues:

> We need to move beyond our old assumptions that it is primarily the students' responsibility to integrate all the disparate parts of an undergraduate education. We must fully grasp that students will learn to integrate deeply and meaningfully only insofar as we design a curriculum that cultivates that; and designing such a curriculum requires that we similarly plan, strategize and execute integratively across the boundaries within our institutions. (p. 32)

Keep in mind that, in the 2019 national survey, only 55% of recent college graduates reported having multiple opportunities during college to reflect on how the different parts of their college experience fit together. And a full 17% reported never having had that opportunity, so college curricula seem to be falling short of this goal. In addition, first-generation students, graduates who took classes mostly online, and graduates who commuted to campus were less likely to have opportunities to reflect for integration.

Bass (2012) argues for a team-based approach to course and curriculum redesign to facilitate integration, with not only faculty participating but also academic support staff. I believe we need to take this team-based approach a step further. After all, on-campus employment, student organizations, and residential life spaces—as only three examples—often are relationship-rich environments that include authentic opportunities for students to transfer and integrate prior knowledge. Barber (2020) also argues for cross-silo collaboration, noting that "college students spend up to 90% of their time outside the classroom in residence halls, at internship sites, on athletic fields, and in part-time or full-time employment" (p. 9). The boundaries we create with institutional reporting structures simply do not reflect our students' lived experiences.

As our students move among these multiple activity systems, how might we—faculty and staff—prepare learners to be more successful boundary-crossers? How might we make their transitions consequential, supporting them not only in their integration of prior and new knowledge but also in employing or developing boundary objects that enable them to positively impact the systems they inhabit? Perkins and Salomon also contributed teaching strategies relevant to these goals. "Hugging" strategies facilitate the development of practiced habits needed for low road transfer, and "bridging" strategies foster the mindful abstraction used in high road transfer. In the sections that follow, I share examples of hugging and bridging strategies and "boundary objects" that facilitate students' consequential boundary-crossing.

Promoting Transfer and Integration in the Classroom

Strategies for promoting transfer and integration draw on the other five key practices. The National Research Council volume *How People Learn* notes, "People must achieve a threshold of initial learning that is sufficient to support transfer" (Bransford et al., 2000, p. 235). Students therefore need opportunities to develop the prior knowledge they'll eventually transfer and integrate. *How People Learn* also highlights "the importance of helping students monitor their learning so that they seek feedback and actively evaluate their strategies and current levels of understanding" (p. 236), reiterating the importance of developing feedback communities.

Similarly, the *Elon Statement on Writing Transfer* suggests, "Practices that promote writing transfer include . . . explicitly modeling transfer-focused thinking and the application of metacognitive awareness as a conscious and explicit part of a process of learning" (Center for Engaged Learning, 2015, para. 26). Reflection is a key part of transfer-focused thinking since reflection helps learners make meaning of their experiences, and *metacognitive*

TABLE 7.1
Transfer-Focused Thinking Prompts

Reflecting Back . . .	*Bridging Forward . . .*
When I approach this type of project, I draw on . . .	This project required you to develop/practice [specific knowledge]; I find myself using that knowledge when I . . .
In the last assignment, you needed to apply what you know about [specific knowledge]; this assignment is similar but requires you to adapt that knowledge in this way . . .	The [specific knowledge] you practiced in this assignment will be relevant when . . .
We did project X first because we'll need to analyze the data we gathered to prepare our strategy for project Y.	My work with projects like this helped me demonstrate that I was qualified for advancement; I was able to . . .

reflection helps students evaluate their prior knowledge, adapt it for new situations, and monitor their success with those adaptions or applications, as discussed in chapter 6. Table 7.1 offers examples of transfer-focused thinking that staff and faculty can model for students. These types of transfer-focused thinking prompts can serve as hugging strategies when they illustrate that new tasks draw on students' practiced habits and as bridging strategies when students have opportunities to reflect more abstractly about how they might adapt knowledge, skills, and strategies for future goals.

Of course, learning experiences should embrace all of students' prior and concurrent experiences, not only those associated with institutions of learning. Marcus, for example, is one of approximately 8 million adult learners (i.e., 25 or older) and one of approximately 1.2 million military students (i.e., veterans or active duty or reserve soldiers; Renn & Reason, 2021). His 4 years of active duty included 24 weeks (~6 months) of training and an additional 3.5 years of on-the-job experience in the United States and abroad, making it likely that he has job and life experiences relevant to many of his college courses—if he's invited to draw on that prior knowledge. Figure 7.2 offers a reminder that learners should be encouraged to draw on their prior and concurrent experiences, in addition to their classroom learning experiences, as they integrate their learning and think about how it prepares them for their future experiences—both in and beyond college.

Typically, a student's current learning experience with a specific faculty or staff member—whether an individual class, a workplace setting, or a student organization—accounts for only a very small portion of their knowledge base; their prior knowledge and experiences include an array of other concurrent learning experiences that they can integrate and transfer to both

Figure 7.2. Influences on students' current learning experience that collectively could contribute to future experiences.

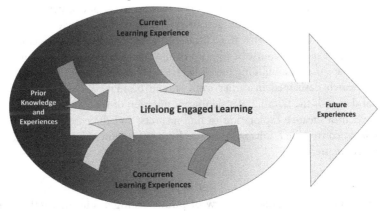

TABLE 7.2

Transfer-Focused Questions for Integration Across Experiences

Reflecting Back . . .	*Bridging Forward . . .*
As you approach this project, what skills and strategies do you think you can draw from your past experiences, your other courses, and your other current day-to-day activities, including your contributions to campus organizations or work?	This project required you to develop/practice [specific knowledge]; how might you use that knowledge in your other courses this term, in your campus activities, or at work?
Where in your daily life have you encountered similar ideas or strategies? How do they relate to our current discussion/project?	In the next week, when or where could you try out this concept/strategy in your daily life?

current and future learning. Table 7.2 shares transfer-focused questions that invite students to integrate and transfer their knowledge from the prior and from their concurrent experiences.

Promoting Transfer and Integration in Capstone Courses

Capstone courses present one potential space to systematically design learning experiences to foster integration of learning. The Boyer Commission's 1998 report, *Reinventing Undergraduate Education: A Blueprint for America's Research Universities,* called for students' education to "culminate with a capstone experience" (p. 27). While not a new concept—since capstones have existed since the late 1800s—the Boyer Commission advocated a renewed focus on promoting integration:

> The final semester(s) should focus on a major project and utilize to the fullest the research and communication skills learned in the previous semesters. In order to ensure that the educational experience is drawn together, the student needs a course at the end of the curriculum that corresponds to the capstone of a building or the keystone of an arch. . . . All the skills of research developed in earlier work should be marshaled in a project that demands the framing of a significant question or set of questions, the research or creative exploration to find answers, and the communication skills to convey the results to audiences both expert and uninitiated in the subject matter. (p. 27)

Unfortunately, this vision has not yet been realized for the majority of college students. In a systematic review of public-facing academic catalogs and other program documents at 487 colleges and universities in Australia, the

United Kingdom, and the United States, a 2018–2020 research seminar team identified only 11% (55) that explicitly required a capstone experience (Bean et al., 2023). Among the U.S. institutions in the study, only 15% (48 of the 319) required a capstone (Bean et al., 2023). In the 2020 National Survey of Student Engagement, 42% of seniors reported participating in culminating senior experiences (NSSE, n.d.), but that suggests that, without required capstone experiences, over half of college students do not have this critical opportunity for integration of their learning.

When students do encounter capstones, their expectations for the experience may differ from faculty expectations. Another 2018–2020 research seminar team studied student and faculty perceptions of capstones at four institutions in the United States, Canada, and the United Kingdom. Students and faculty often prioritized different values, skills/competencies, and attitudes when asked about the purposes for capstone experiences (Vale et al., 2020). For example, 52% of humanities students surveyed thought capstones should have a career orientation, while only 17% of humanities faculty identified that purpose. Meanwhile, 90% of engineering faculty thought students should develop professional attitudes as an outcome of a capstone experience, while only 47% of engineering students identified that goal (Vale et al., 2020, p. 4). These differing perspectives highlight the need for alignment in the communication about capstones so that students, faculty, staff, and administrators have a shared understanding of the goals of capstones and the pathways into them (Ketcham et al., 2022, 2023).

Ideally, capstone courses provide students with prompts to integrate learning from multiple prior and concurrent experiences, some degree of agency in shaping their culminating experience, and opportunities to apply their knowledge to real-world situations (Ketcham et al., 2022). They can take a range of forms while meeting these goals. For example, another 2018–2020 seminar participant, David Lewis, describes a variety of capstone experiences for bioscience majors, ranging from research projects to commercial or technical reports to civic and societal capstones with service- or community-based learning components (in Lewis et al., 2023).

Promoting Transfer and Integration via Course-Based ePortfolios

In addition to being a tool to promote reflection, as discussed in chapter 6, ePortfolios can function as a tool to promote integration of learning. Faculty at Bronx Community College use ePortfolios in a first-year seminar course to "empower students to bridge the gap between their personal and academic experiences and to draw visible connections between their college education and their professional future" (Getman-Eraso & Culkin, 2018, p. 33). Using an ePortfolio as a tool for integration in students' first year has the potential to highlight the value of their "prior" and to introduce students to inquiry, reflection, and integration strategies (e.g., Eynon & Gambino, 2017) they can continue to hone throughout college.

Sandra Bell, Frederick T. Evers, Shannon Murray, and Margaret Anne Smith (2023) describe using course-based ePortfolios as a culminating or capstone experience in multiple disciplinary contexts at four different institutions. Evers, for example, describes using portfolios in a sociology and anthropology course to help students document the skills they've developed and showcase those skills for potential employers. Similarly, Murray uses ePortfolios in a "Capstone in Arts" course to prompt students' development of a work philosophy and documentation of their relevant skills.

At the University of South Carolina, students who wish to graduate with a leadership distinction enroll in a one-credit senior seminar (or alternately follow a structured advisement pathway) to develop an integrative ePortfolio that connects their course-based and out-of-class experiences (Van Scoy et al., 2018). Students share "key insights . . . that articulate how your within-the-classroom (WTC) and beyond-the-classroom (BTC) experiences influenced one another in order to create a change in your professional or life practices" and curate "artifacts" that support their key insight statements (University of South Carolina, n.d., p. 2).

Across these examples, ePortfolios function as a *tool* to facilitate integration. Combining the technology with mentoring and other developmental relationships (chapter 3), iterative opportunities for feedback (chapter 4), and scaffolded reflection (chapter 6) shifts this tool to a HIP done well. By drawing on these key practices for fostering engaged learning, faculty using ePortfolios in their classrooms create opportunities for students to draw on "the prior" (chapter 2), and often to integrate learning from their connections to broader contexts (chapter 5) with their course-based experiences.

Promoting Transfer and Integration Beyond the Classroom

Contexts beyond the classroom often inherently—though not always explicitly—invite students to transfer and integrate knowledge from multiple prior and concurrent contexts. As Peter Felten (2017) notes,

> Many HIPs immerse students in settings that require proactive knowledge because they do *not* explicitly cue students to apply specific content or skills to address a well-defined problem. Instead they present open-ended situations that students must navigate with far less guidance than they receive in a typical classroom. (p. 52, emphasis in original)

This low-cue context (in contrast to a classroom's high-cue context) may present challenges for students trying to determine what relevant prior knowledge they have, yet the lack of explicit cues also could enable students to consider a broader array of prior knowledge. If a context doesn't explicitly cue me to use knowledge from my math classes, for instance, I might also draw relevant knowledge from research experiences, visual design courses, and work experiences. Felten (2017) focuses his discussion on UR, learning communities, service-learning/community-based learning, and internships, but his observation also applies to other contexts for learning beyond the classroom.

Promoting Transfer and Integration via UR

Mentored UR often provides opportunities for integration and transfer of learning as students draw on "the prior" developed in multiple courses. Undergraduate researchers, for example, might draw on skills learned in first-year writing and subsequent courses in the discipline as they search library databases for relevant scholarship on their topic. They might apply research methods introduced in introductory courses in their major and practiced in subsequent courses. While research contexts might be high-cue for prior knowledge developed in disciplinary coursework, they often are low-cue for other prior knowledge (e.g., from general education coursework, minors, cocurricular experiences, etc.). Faculty and staff who adopt the salient practices of mentoring UR (Shanahan et al., 2015) can employ bridging strategies to facilitate student transfer and integration of learning by devoting time to strategic preplanning to learn more about students' relevant prior knowledge and experiences, offering frequent feedback via one-to-one mentoring, and creating intentional opportunities for peer mentoring, during which peers and near peers might draw attention to other shared learning experiences that are relevant to the research.

Promoting Transfer and Integration With Transfer-Bridging ePortfolios

While ePortfolios can be course-based tools for promoting integrative learning, they also can span courses and other experiences. As Bass (2012) notes, ePortfolios "allow students to organize learning around the learner rather than around courses or the curriculum. Once intended for assessment or employment presentation, e-portfolios are being reinvented as integrative spaces across the undergraduate experience" (p. 26). For this reason, Bret Eynon and Laura Gambino (2017) advocate that "students use ePortfolios to bring together work from multiple contexts, consider the relationship

TABLE 7.3
Examples of Integrative ePortfolio Projects

Institution/ Program	ePortfolio Integrates Student Learning From . . .	Year Students Complete ePortfolio	Learn More
LaGuardia Community College (CUNY)	Coursework and cocurricular experiences	Started in first-year seminar and developed throughout coursework	Bhika et al., 2018
University at Buffalo	General education coursework	Typically during third year	Van Zile-Tamsen et al., 2023
Elon University professional writing and rhetoric major	Major coursework, related outside electives or minors, internship(s), and undergraduate research	Constructed recursively during studies, with external assessment of a senior year version	Moore et al., 2018

between their classrooms and their lives outside of class, and construct new identities as learners" (p. 35). Table 7.3 highlights examples of integrative ePortfolio projects.

The ePortfolio examples that span multiple courses or college experiences reflect what Kathleen Blake Yancey (2017) calls a "transfer-bridging portfolio" (p. 44). By scaffolding portfolio development over time, these ePortfolio programs create space for recursive reflection and integration of learning, not bounded by the high-cue context of a specific course. According to the 2019 national survey, however, only 18% of recent college graduates reported developing an ePortfolio during college (CEL/Elon Poll, 2019). Colleges can increase these rates by integrating ePortfolios into existing institutional structures. For example, linking ePortfolio development to academic advising, with students sharing an additional ePortfolio artifact and reflective component each time they meet with their advisor, gives time and space to the scaffolded development of ePortfolios with frequent opportunities for feedback (Moore et al., 2018). Alternatively, on-campus employment also can function as a site for scaffolded ePortfolio development, particularly if supervisors encourage student employees to add artifacts each semester that showcase their evolving professional development and take opportunities to offer feedback and promote reflection.

Promoting Transfer and Integration in On-Campus Employment

As previously discussed, students' supervisors are well positioned to facilitate students' reflection, a key practice for promoting transfer and integration of learning. With guided reflection, supervisors can invite students to apply and practice relevant course-based learning, as well as "the prior" that students develop during their involvement in campus organizations and other concurrent experiences. Supervisors also can give feedback on how well students have adapted prior knowledge for a new context or task and support metacognitive reflection on how to adjust strategies for future tasks in—and beyond—the work context. In other words, student employment is a natural setting for modeling transfer-focused thinking, and practices like Iowa GROW center reflection for integration.

Promoting Transfer and Integration in Living-Learning Communities

Living-learning communities (LLCs) offer an additional space to promote integration of learning. As Jennifer Eidum and Lara Lomika (2023), two participants in the 2017–2019 research seminar on residential learning communities, highlight, "an LLC could provide experiential programming that provides students with the opportunity to focus on interdisciplinary and interprofessional collaboration across disciplines, promote intellectual development, and foster community learning" (p. 8). Because LLCs are low-cue, they may not explicitly cue students to transfer knowledge from specific prior and concurrent experiences, instead prompting students to integrate from multiple curricular, cocurricular, and extracurricular contexts.

Implications and Recommendations for Individual Faculty and Staff

Promoting students' integration and transfer of learning begins with the other five key practices. Faculty and staff can support students by inviting them to share "the prior" they bring to each new situation, helping students develop a practiced habit of inventorying their relevant knowledge and experience— the "prior" available to integrate and transfer. Developing and maintaining helping relationships with students ensures they have someone to turn to for academic and professional development support as they learn boundary-crossing strategies—first as they move among courses and concurrent college experiences and eventually as they pursue professional, civic, and personal goals after college. Offering frequent, actionable feedback contributes to a campus's feedback culture and enables students to learn from their attempts to integrate and adapt their "prior" to new contexts. Prompting reflection invites students to reflect on what's working, to anticipate how what they're learning might transfer to future tasks, and to develop metacognitive habits for lifelong learning.

The outcomes of each of these practices therefore are additive, building toward promoting students' integration and transfer of learning. As a result, the collective practices do not necessarily have to be time-intensive. When students have a network of faculty and staff collectively engaging the six key practices, the in-class exit writes inviting students to brainstorm relevant prior knowledge, the quick conversations with supervisors who offer describe–evaluate–suggest feedback, and the encouragement from advisors to reflect on how curricular and cocurricular experiences are preparing students for future goals collectively enable students to develop and practice boundary-crossing strategies.

Faculty and staff can contribute to this community-wide effort by considering the following:

- When and how often do I invite students to explicitly make connections between what they're doing with me and what they're learning in (other) classes this semester, courses in their major, and courses in general education?
- How might I design assignments or projects to explicitly encourage students to practice skills or strategies they've learned in other contexts?
- What do I know about "the prior" that students bring to their work with me? How might I engage students in making visible connections between their prior knowledge and experiences and their work with me?

Implications and Recommendations for Program and Institution Leaders

Programs and institutions that value integration and transfer of learning should provide professional development in support of these goals. For example, faculty teaching capstone experiences can benefit from workshops on aligning their course design with program and institutional goals for the capstone (Ketcham et al., 2022). Programs can amplify this alignment when they map curricular content to understand which courses introduce knowledge and strategies and which offer opportunities to practice and build on this prior knowledge; capstone faculty then have a roadmap for students' pathways to the capstone and the curricular experiences students could integrate in a well-designed capstone.

While this chapter showcases several ePortfolio examples, ePortfolios done well also require significant professional development, and ePortfolio mentors need time to engage in iterative feedback cycles with students to scaffold students' reflection and integration. A technology platform is not sufficient to implement a truly high-impact ePortfolio practice. Institutions also must invest in the faculty and staff who mentor students' portfolio development and revision.

Moreover, as the 2019 national survey and NSSE data show, students do not have universal or equitable access to educational practices that facilitate transfer and integration of learning. Institutions that believe all students should have access to these key practices need to embed them throughout institutional structures, ideally in both curricular contexts and other central campus activities, so that all students have multiple opportunities to practice transferring and integrating their learning.

8

CONCLUSION

Implementing High-Quality Engaged Learning

A staff member, a faculty member, and an administrator walk into the campus (coffee) bar . . . Maya, Delsin, and Coburn had approached two of them with concerns about equitable access to some of the campus's premier learning experiences that are heavily promoted to potential students. Maya realized that she had benefited from early and recurring access to undergraduate research (UR) experiences, but many of her peers had missed out on those opportunities. She'd even been asked to participate in a photo shoot with her research mentor to showcase UR in an admissions brochure. Yet when she told her roommate about the photo shoot, her roommate shared that she wanted to participate in UR but wasn't sure how to find a mentor who would work with her. During their next weekly meeting, Maya had asked her faculty mentor what the university was doing to help other students engage in research.

Delsin and Coburn had asked their Keepers of the Fire advisor whether he knew of any students from the reservation who had studied abroad. They both were interested, but they wondered if they'd encounter the same biases in other parts of the world that they often endured in the United States. Would they be treated as novelties? Experience new forms of prejudices? Or was there someplace they could study abroad where they'd feel like they fit in—even as they explored new-to-them places and cultures? Delsin shared that, while he wanted to see more of the world, he also was a bit leery of the whole idea of study away. He remembered college students from another state coming to the reservation to complete service projects; his *gagu* (grandma) had expressed appreciation for their help, but he sometimes felt like he was a tourist attraction. He didn't want to study abroad if it would make other people feel that way.

Maya's research mentor and Delsin and Coburn's organization advisor each had asked their administrative colleague to meet to talk through the students' questions, knowing the administrator was interested in increasing participation in the campus's experiential learning activities. Their emails had landed in the administrator's inbox on the same day, amplifying her own concerns about offering equitable, high-quality experiences, so she invited both colleagues to join her for coffee.

As they sipped their drinks, the educators began to share their stories, compiling more questions for each other:

- Who was participating in the campus's high-profile high-impact practices (HIPs), like UR, internships, and study away, and who wasn't? Among students who hadn't participated, why hadn't they? Were they encountering other opportunities that fostered engaged learning?
- How could they increase access to HIPs—and ensure that as more students participated, they still had high-quality experiences?
- Even if they resolved access challenges, some HIPs might not be a good fit for students' personal situations or professional goals, so what could the campus do to ensure all students had learning experiences that featured the six key practices for fostering engaged learning?
- Meaningful learning experiences aren't isolated to HIPs, so how could the campus identify, enhance, assess, and celebrate other existing learning experiences in and beyond the classroom that embody the six key practices?
- How could they tap the campus's values and strengths to ensure all students had equitable, high-quality learning experiences?

This concluding chapter revisits why efforts to foster engaged learning must attend to equity and then offers heuristics for prioritizing key takeaways and implications from the previous chapters in order to implement or enrich engaged learning in classrooms, programs, and institutions. By attending to the six key practices, each member of a college or university community can contribute to scaling equitable access to high-quality engaged learning.

Equity in Engaged Learning

All students deserve equitable opportunities for engaged learning. Unfortunately, the 2019 survey of recent college graduates suggests that many students have limited exposure to the six key practices that could deepen their learning and contribute to their persistence and success. Table 8.1 consolidates many of the survey findings shared in the previous chapters.

TABLE 8.1

Recent College Graduates' Experiences With the Six Key Practices

During Your College/University Experience, to What Extent Did You Encounter . . .	*Never*	*Once*	*Multiple Times*
Faculty who asked you to draw on *prior experiences* when you learned new things	14.5%	26.6%	58.9%
Meaningful *relationships* with faculty or staff	17.3%	30.7%	52.0%
Meaningful *relationships* with other students	11.5%	21.8%	66.6%
Feedback from peers to guide your work before you submitted a final version	14.0%	28.0%	58.0%
Feedback from faculty/staff to guide your work before you submitted a final version	9.9%	24.0%	66.1%
Feedback from faculty/staff on a submitted, final project	7.1%	21.1%	71.8%
Practice with real-world applications of what you were learning (e.g., *connections to broader contexts*)	12.2%	26.6%	61.3%
Opportunities to *reflect* on how what you were learning would apply to your future (e.g., *transfer*)	10.8%	23.2%	65.9%
Opportunities to *reflect* on how the different parts of your college experience fit together (e.g., *integration*)	17.2%	27.6%	55.2%

Note. From CEL/Elon Poll, 2019.

HIPs done well can be sites for implementing these six key practices. Reflecting in 2013 on HIPs research conducted subsequent to his paradigm-shifting 2008 publication, George Kuh noted:

> On balance, the patterns of positive results are generally consistent across all studies (Brownell & Swaner, 2010), even though most of the research about HIPs does not take into account the structural aspects of the program or practice or how well specific high-impact practices are implemented. That is, as practitioners know, some service-learning courses are "better" than others, especially if there are frequent instructor-mediated discussions among students and shared personal reflection about the relevance of course readings to what they are encountering in the field. Similarly, some first-year seminars and learning communities are organized in ways that more effectively compel students to reach high standards of performance while providing ample feedback along the way from peers as well as teachers. (pp. 1–2)

In other words, the activities we collectively designate as HIPs are not automatically high-impact. Some instances of the practices we know as HIPs are implemented in ways that achieve characteristics of HIPs associated with desired learning gains, but some are not. Kuh, Ken O'Donnell, and Carol Geary Schneider (2017) extend this caution in their 10-year retrospective on HIPs, noting, "the positive influence of participating in a HIP is likely a function of multiple effective educational practices that are characteristics of a HIP *done well* " (p. 11, emphasis added). They further suggest that given the potential outcomes for learners, HIPs should be broadly implemented "with consistency, fidelity and reliability. Yet in some important ways such adoption is still ahead of us; there are significant challenges in terms of scaling and insuring quality" (p. 13). And without that consistent quality—without ensuring each implementation of a designated practice embodies the eight characteristics that make it "high-impact" or "done well"—the practice may not lead to the anticipated learning outcomes that prompt institutions to adopt HIPs.

Moreover, access to HIPs remains uneven—and inequitable. Table 8.2 shares recent data on participation rates in designated HIPs. Looking across these HIPs, students are most likely to participate in service- or

TABLE 8.2
Participation Rates for Select High-Impact Practices

High-Impact Practice	*Participation Rate*	
	CEL/Elon Poll Survey of U.S. Graduates (2019/2021)	*National Survey of Student Engagement—2020 Seniors*
Internship, field experience, or work placement	52%/50%	50%
Service-learning or community-engaged learning	35%/36%	59%
Capstone project or culminating experience	32%/32%	42%
Undergraduate Research	32%/32%	23%
Study Abroad	19%/20%	14%
ePortfolio	18%/18%	N/A
Learning Community	N/A	21%

Note. From CEL/Elon Poll, 2019, 2021; NSSE, n.d.

community-based learning, but in these data sets, only 59% of seniors—at most—reported having this experience during their college education (NSSE, n.d.). Kuh et al. (2017) share that "first generation, transfer students, and African-American and Latino students [are] least likely to participate" in HIPs (p. 12). These same learner groups perceive deeper learning gains when they participate in HIPs than their peers who do not participate, with those perceived gains increasing as these students participate in additional HIPs (Finley & McNair, 2013). Yet the students who often report the greatest self-perceived gains from HIPs typically have the least access to them.

Digging deeper into data on internship and co-op participation certainly illustrates this trend. For the past 20 years, male students consistently have accounted for 44% of undergraduate enrollment in the United States, and in a 2018 enrollment analysis, 52.2% of U.S. college students identified as white (Renn & Reason, 2021). Yet in the executive summary of their *2021 Internship & Co-Op Survey Report*, the National Association of Colleges and Employers (2021a) suggests, "Overall, men account for the majority of interns and co-ops of responding organizations, and the majority of those taking part in such programs are white" (p. 3). Specifically, in the 2021 survey, 57.6% of interns identified as male, and 62% identified as white (NACE, 2021b). Both percentages increase in reference to co-ops (67.5% and 71%, respectively; NACE, 2021b). Asian American students account for 13.9% of interns, African American students for 8.2%, and Hispanic American students for 7.3% (NACE, 2021b).

Given the limited and uneven access to high-impact educational experiences, higher education faculty, staff, and administrators who care about equitable education need to refocus attention on the characteristics of meaningful learning. Collectively, the six key practices for fostering engaged learning prepare students to identify and apply relevant prior knowledge, work with diverse others, request and use feedback, make connections, reflect on their abilities, and contribute to resolving the world's wicked problems by integrating or transferring their "prior." As a result, enacting these key practices ultimately is an act of social justice to ensure all students have meaningful learning experiences that enable them to actively and intentionally participate in their own lifelong learning and to contribute meaningfully to their communities and workplaces.

Interconnected Key Practices

Although the prior chapters address each key practice individually, their associated outcomes increase exponentially when educators approach them as interconnected practices (see Figure 8.1). Students are better prepared

Figure 8.1. Interconnected key practices for fostering engaged learning.

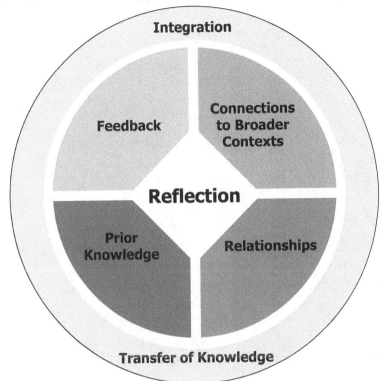

to connect their learning to broader contexts when they can reflect on and integrate their prior knowledge and experiences. Similarly, students often process feedback more effectively when they have established relationships with the peers, staff, and faculty who are offering suggestions for improvement. Reflection helps students make meaning in specific contexts, and metacognitive reflection helps them take stock of learning strategies for lifelong and lifewide learning. Collectively, the six key practices foster engaged learners who are prepared to participate actively and intentionally in their own learning, not only at discrete moments but rather as an ongoing, lifelong activity.

Low-Investment Strategies to Enact the Key Practices

Because the key practices are interconnected, intentionally implementing even one of the practices creates a foundation for subsequent implementation of the others. I encourage faculty and staff to consider what's feasible

Figure 8.2. Prioritizing reflection also supports other key practices.

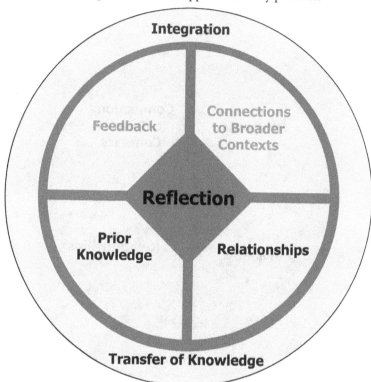

and might have the most immediate effect in their contexts. For example, if you supervise student employees and begin a recurring reflection initiative like Iowa GROW, your primary focus might be on reflection, but you also are positioning yourself to deepen your relationships with your student employees, to identify and build on their prior knowledge and experience, and to promote integration and transfer of knowledge (see Figure 8.2). In a 5-year plan, these other key practices could become foci for years 2, 3, and 4, allowing an office team to deliberately add one key practice each year.

If you teach a first-year course, you might initially focus on "the prior" and reflection, helping students practice making their prior knowledge visible to themselves and others, as well as reflect on the relevance of that prior knowledge for new tasks and contexts. Since prior knowledge is a cornerstone for other key practices and reflection is a facilitator, that pairing sets up subsequent attention to integration and transfer of knowledge (see Figure 8.3).

Figure 8.3. Focusing on prior knowledge as a cornerstone and reflection as a facilitator.

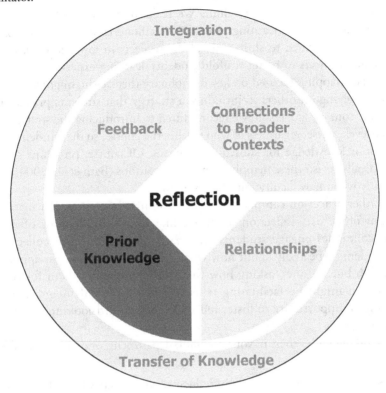

This prioritization isn't intended to suggest that you should assume other colleagues will attend to the other key practices; rather it's intended to suggest that you can add key practices to your repertoire incrementally over time. As you prioritize key practices to enact, consider the following:

- What key practices do I already use, and where?
- Could I extend my use of a key practice to other contexts where I'm not currently enacting it?
- Which key practice could I most easily add to my work with students? Which key practices do I need more support (e.g., professional development, buy-in from others) to enact?

Program-Level Strategies to Enact the Key Practices

Programs can increase the likelihood of all students experiencing the key practices by doing a program-wide assessment of how and where they're implemented. For example, in the professional writing major in which I teach, my colleagues and I did a quick mapping of the types of assignments we included across the curriculum. We realized that we collectively were overrelying on service-learning projects to facilitate connections to broader contexts and decided to shift some of the projects in lower-level classes to case-based projects to better scaffold students' learning experiences. A similar course mapping focused on key disciplinary theories highlighted that we all were relying on others to introduce a strategy that students practiced in multiple courses; as a result, we recommitted to introducing the strategy in a lower-level course, regardless of who teaches the course, so that students have that prior knowledge for subsequent courses. Of course, programs should periodically revisit these mappings and conversations (Bath et al., 2004), particularly when new faculty join the program.

Other offices on campus can conduct similar mappings. For instance, if your office uses reflection questions like Iowa GROW, how often do your colleagues engage students with each question? If you collectively ask students repeatedly about how what they're learning in class applies to their job but no one's asking how their job is preparing them for future goals, you might be facilitating reflection in support of integration but missing an opportunity to foster reflection for forward-looking transfer of knowledge.

Working with others in your program, department, or division, consider:

- What knowledge are we introducing, when, and where? How do we explicitly draw on that prior knowledge in subsequent courses, projects, or activities?
- How are we fostering relationships, including peer-to-peer and near-peer relationships, within our program, office, or division?
- How often do we provide feedback to students to guide their learning? Who else could we engage in offering frequent, meaningful feedback?
- How do we frame connections to broader contexts? Is our office/division tackling wicked tendencies that students could connect their course-based learning to? Are we helping students connect the work they're doing with us to wicked problems in the broader community or profession?
- How and when do we engage students in reflection? How might we help students develop metacognitive reflection practices for lifelong learning?
- How and when do we invite students to transfer and integrate their knowledge for application in new contexts or for new audiences and purposes?

Institution-Wide Strategies to Enact the Key Practices

Just as programs or offices can map how they are enacting the key practices, administrators can facilitate institutional scans to identify opportunities for and potential barriers to enhancing use of the key practices across campus. Involving students in this process increases the likelihood that resulting mappings reflect not only intentions for fostering engaged learning but also students' lived experiences as they move among activity systems on campus.

Although any faculty or staff member can implement the key practices, as with any educational initiative to support equitable, high-quality engaged learning, institutions can support faculty/staff implementation by:

- providing professional development in support of each key practice
- allocating resources (including time) to program-level assessments of and initiatives in support of the key practices
- minimizing barriers to cross-campus collaborations in support of the key practices

The book website includes materials to support professional development activities. Of course, institutions shouldn't overlook local expertise. If an institutional scan identifies programs or offices that excel in their implementation of a key practice, those local faculty or staff might be well positioned to help colleagues brainstorm how to enact a practice in *your* institutional context with *your* students.

Large-scale initiatives like the quality enhancement plans associated with some reaccreditation processes can offer significant resources for assessing and enhancing campus-wide use of the key practices, but smaller-scale initiatives can have a comparable impact for individual programs or offices. For example, a recurring course (re)design workshop could help individual faculty systematically integrate the key practices throughout the courses they personally teach. A department retreat could give a program or office time to map their collective implementation of key practices and plan adjustments. And an ongoing community of practice could facilitate implementation and assessment of the key practices and foster research about the impact of their use on campus.

Regardless of how campuses support faculty and staff implementation of the key practices, that support needs to extend to annual reviews and promotions. Allocating space in review processes for faculty and staff to share how they are facilitating relationships, framing connections to broader contexts, or enacting other key practices enables supervisors to celebrate successes.

Moreover, this type of periodic reflection about individual use of the key practices opens up opportunities for faculty and staff to set goals and action plans to enhance their use of the key practices in ways that will be recognized by the institution. If annual reviews do not recognize how faculty and staff are contributing to students' engaged learning, the reviews can become a barrier to campus-wide enactment of the key practices.

Institutional scans may reveal other potential barriers—policies or practices that deter faculty/staff collaboration across the same boundaries that students routinely navigate, staffing practices that impinge on developing and maintaining relationships or that complicate program efforts to build on and integrate students' prior knowledge, and so forth. Few campuses, if any, could eliminate all potential barriers immediately, but cataloging these types of barriers allows institutions to construct strategic plans to reduce barriers to fostering engaged learning over time.

Ultimately, the institutional benefits to supporting campus-wide implementation of the key practices are monumental. Collectively, the interconnected key practices for fostering engaged learning prepare students—*all* students—to be active participants in their lifelong learning, more satisfied with their college experiences and better prepared for their personal, professional, and civic futures.

REFERENCES

Abbot, S., Bellwoar, H., & Hall, E. E. (2020). The importance of reciprocity in mentoring: Benefits and challenges. In D. DelliCarpini, J. Fishman, & J. Greer (Eds.), *The Naylor Report on undergraduate research in writing studies* (pp. 45–48). Parlor Press.

Addy, T. M., Dube, D., Mitchell, K. A., & SoRelle, M. E. (2021). *What inclusive instructors do: Principles and practices for excellence in college teaching.* Stylus.

Adler-Kassner, L., Clark, I., Robertson, L., Taczak, K., & Yancey, K. B. (2016/2017). Assembling knowledge: The role of threshold concepts in facilitating transfer. In C.A. Anson & J. L. Moore (Eds.), *Critical transitions: Writing and the question of transfer* (pp. 17–47). The WAC Clearinghouse/University Press of Colorado. https://doi.org/10.37514/PER-B.2016.0797.2.01

Ambrose, S. A., Bridges, M. W., DiPietro, M., Lovett, M. C., & Norman, M. K. (2010). *How learning works: Seven research-based principles for smart teaching.* Jossey-Bass.

Arendale, D. R. (2010). *Access at the crossroads: Learning assistance in higher education* (ASHE Higher Education Report, Vol. 35, no. 6). Jossey-Bass. https://doi.org/10.1002/aehe.3506

Ash, S. L., & Clayton, P. H. (2004). The articulated learning: An approach to guided reflection and assessment. *Innovative Higher Education, 29*(2), 137–154. https://doi.org/10.1023/B:IHIE.0000048795.84634.4a

Ash, S. L., & Clayton, P. H. (2009). Generating, deepening, and documenting learning: The power of critical reflection in applied learning. *Journal of Applied Learning in Higher Education, 1*(Fall), 25–48.

Astin, A. W. (1993). *What matters in college? Four critical years revisited.* Jossey-Bass.

Balester, V. (2012). How writing rubrics fail: Toward a multicultural model. In A. B. Inoue & M. Poe (Eds.), *Race and writing assessment* (pp. 63–77). Peter Lang.

Barber, J. P. (2020). *Facilitating the integration of learning: Five research-based practices to help college students connect learning across disciplines and lived experience.* Stylus.

Bass, R. (2012). Disrupting ourselves: The problem of learning in higher education. *Educause Review, 47*(2), 23–33. https://er.educause.edu/articles/2012/3/disrupting-ourselves-the-problem-of-learning-in-higher-education

Bass, R., & Eynon, B. (2016). *Open and integrative: Designing liberal education for the new digital ecosystem.* Association of American Colleges and Universities.

Bath, D., Smith, C., Stein, S., & Swann, R. (2004). Beyond mapping and embedding graduate attributes: Bringing together quality assurance and action learning to create a validated and living curriculum. *Higher Education Research & Development, 23*(3), 313–328. https://doi.org/10.1080/0729436042000235427

Beach, K. (2003). Consequential transitions: A developmental view of knowledge propagation through social organizations. In T. Tuomi-Gröhn & Y. Engeström (Eds.), *Between school and work: New perspectives on transfer and boundary-crossing* (pp. 39–61). Emerald Group.

Bean, J., Beaudoin, C., von der Heidt, T., Lewis, D., & Van Zile-Tamsen, C. (2023). Frames, definitions, and drivers: A multinational study of institutionally required undergraduate capstones. In C. Ketcham, A. Weaver, & J. L. Moore (Eds.), *Cultivating capstones: Designing high-quality culminating experiences for student learning* (pp. 27–39). Stylus.

Bell, S., Evers, F. T., Murray, S., & Smith, M. A. (2023). Adapting a capstone: Projects and portfolios across four courses and three institutions. In C. Ketcham, A. Weaver, & J. L. Moore (Eds.), *Cultivating capstones: Designing high-quality culminating experiences for student learning* (pp. 113–122). Stylus.

Berdrow, I., Cruise, R., Levintova, E., Smith, S., Boudon, L., Paracka, D., & Worley, P. M. (2020). Exploring patterns of student global learning choices: A multi-institutional analysis. In N. Namaste & A. Sturgill (Eds.), *Mind the gap: Global learning at home and abroad* (pp. 55–69). Stylus.

Bergmann, L. S., & Zepernick, J. (2007). Disciplinarity and transfer: Students' perceptions of learning to write. *Writing Program Administration, 31*(1–2), 124–149.

Bhika, R., Quish, E., & Hofmann, E. (2018). Critical junctures: Professional development in an evolving ePortfolio landscape. In B. Eynon & L. M. Gambino (Eds.), *Catalyst in action: Case studies of high-impact ePortfolio practice* (pp. 125–140). Stylus.

Bialka, C. S., & Havlik, S. A. (2016). Partners in learning: Exploring two transformative university and high school service-learning partnerships. *Journal of Experiential Education, 39*(3), 220–237. https://doi.org/10.1177/1053825916640539

Bleakney, J., Carpenter, R., Dvorak, K., Rosinski, P., & Whiddon, S. (2020). How course-embedded consultants and faculty perceive the benefits of course-embedded writing consultant programs. *WLN: A Journal of Writing Center Scholarship, 44*(7–8), 10–17. https://www.wlnjournal.org/archives/v44/44.7-8.pdf

Bleakney, J., Mattison, M., & Ryan, J. (2019). "I was kind of angry": Understanding resistance to feedback in two tutor education courses. *PRAXIS: A Writing Center Journal, 17*(1). http://www.praxisuwc.com/171-bleakney

Blum, S. D. (Ed.). (2020). Just one change (Just kidding): Ungrading and its necessary accompaniments. In *Ungrading: Why rating students undermines learning (and what to do instead)* (pp. 53–73). West Virginia University Press.

Blythe, S. (2016/2017). Attending to the subject in writing transfer and adaptation. In C. M. Anson & J. L. Moore (Eds.), *Critical transitions: Writing and the question of transfer* (pp. 49–68). The WAC Clearinghouse/University Press of Colorado. https://doi.org/10.37514/PER-B.2016.0797.2.02

Boud, D., Keogh, R., & Walker, D. (Eds.). (1985a). Introduction: What is reflection in learning? In *Reflection: Turning experience into learning* (pp. 7–17). Routledge.

Boud, D., Keogh, R., & Walker, D. (1985b). Promoting reflection in learning: A model. In D. Boud, R. Keogh, & D. Walker (Eds.), *Reflection: Turning experience into learning* (pp. 18–40). Routledge.

Bovill, C. (2020). Co-creation in learning and teaching: The case for a whole-class approach in higher education. *Higher Education, 79*, 1023–1037. https://doi.org/10.1007/s10734-019-00453-w

Boyega, J. (2020). *George Floyd protest London speech in full* [Video]. YouTube. https://youtu.be/GGXEB25WdyQ

Boyer Commission on Educating Undergraduates in the Research University. (1998). *Reinventing undergraduate education: A blueprint for America's research universities.* Carnegie Foundation.

Bransford, J. D., Pellegrino, J. W., & Donovan, M. S. (Eds.). (2000). *How people learn: Brain, mind, experience, and school* (Expanded edition). National Academies Press.

Bringle, R., & Hatcher, J. (1999, Summer). Reflection in service-learning: Making meaning of experience. *Educational Horizons*, 179–185. https://digitalcommons.unomaha.edu/slceeval/23

Brownell, J. E., & Swaner, L. E. (2010). *Five high-impact practices: Research on learning outcomes, completion, and quality.* Association of American Colleges and Universities.

Buck, D. (2020a). *Are group assignments a waste of time?* Center for Engaged Learning. https://www.centerforengagedlearning.org/are-group-assignments-a-waste-of-time

Buck, D. (2020b). *Collaborative projects and assignments.* Center for Engaged Learning. https://www.centerforengagedlearning.org/collaborative-projects-and-assignments

Budwig, N., & Jessen-Marshall, A. (2018). Making the case for capstones and signature work. *Peer Review, 20*(2), 4–7.

Center for Engaged Learning. (2015). *Elon statement on writing transfer.* https://www.centerforengagedlearning.org/publications/elon-statements/elon-statement-on-writing-transfer/

Center for Engaged Learning. (2017). *Elon statement on integrating global learning with the university experience: Higher-impact study abroad and off-campus domestic study.* http://www.centerforengagedlearning.org/publications/elon-statements/elon-statement-on-integrating-global-learning/

Center for Engaged Learning. (2020). Mind the Gap *book resources.* https://www.centerforengagedlearning.org/books/mind-the-gap/book-resources/

Center for Engaged Learning/Elon Poll. (2019). *High impact undergraduate experiences and how they matter now: Survey of college graduates, age 18–34.* https://www.elon.edu/u/elon-poll/wp-content/uploads/sites/819/2019/07/2019_7_31-ElonPoll_Report.pdf

Center for Engaged Learning/Elon Poll. (2021). *High impact undergraduate experiences and how they matter now: Survey of college graduates, age 18–34.* http://www.centerforengagedlearning.org/wp-content/uploads/2023/01/Poll_CEL_report_2021-final.pdf

Cheng, M. (2018). Introducing motion-capturing technology into the music practice room as a feedback tool for working towards the precision of rubato. *Journal of Music, Technology & Education, 11*(2), 149–170. https://doi.org/10.1386/jmte.11.2.149_1

Chick, N. L., Karis, T., & Kernahan, C. (2009). Learning from their own learning: How metacognitive and meta-affective reflections enhance learning in race-related courses. *International Journal for the Scholarship of Teaching and Learning*, *3*(1), Article 16. https://doi.org/10.20429/ijsotl.2009.030116

Chickering, A. W., & Gamson, Z. F. (1987, March). Seven principles for good practice in undergraduate education. *American Association for Higher Education Bulletin*, 3–7. https://eric.ed.gov/?id=ED282491

Chickering, A. W., & Gamson, Z. F. (1999, Winter). Development and adaptations of the seven principles for good practice in undergraduate education. In M. D. Svinicki (Ed.), *Teaching and Learning on the Edge of the Millennium: Building on What We Have Learned* (New Directions for Teaching and Learning, no. 80, pp. 75–81). Jossey-Bass.

Cho, K., & MacArthur, C. (2011). Learning by reviewing. *Journal of Educational Psychology*, *103*(1), 73–84. https://psycnet.apa.org/doi/10.1037/a0021950

Cooper, K. M., Haney, B., Krieg, A., & Brownell, S. E. (2017). What's in a name? The importance of students perceiving that an instructor knows their names in a high-enrollment biology classroom. *CBE Life Sciences Education*, *16*(1), Article 8. https://doi.org/10.1187/cbe.16-08-0265

Davis, S. N., Mahatmya, D., Garner, P. W., & Jones, R. M. (2015). Mentoring undergraduate scholars: A pathway to interdisciplinary research? *Mentoring & Tutoring: Partnership in Learning*, *23*(5), 427–440. https://doi.org/10.1080/13611267.2015.1126166

Dewey, J. (1910). *How we think*. Heath.

Dewey, J. (1916/2018). *Democracy and education*. Introduction by Patricia H. Hinchey. Myers Education Press.

Driscoll, D. L. (2011). Connected, disconnected, or uncertain: Student attitudes about future writing contexts and perceptions of transfer from first year writing to the disciplines. *Across the Disciplines*, *8*(2). https://wac.colostate.edu/docs/atd/articles/driscoll2011.pdf

Eidum, J. E., & Lomicka, L. L. (2023). Introduction to faculty engagement in living–learning communities. In J. E. Eidum & L. L. Lomicka (Eds.), *The faculty factor: Developing faculty engagement with living–learning communities* (pp. 3–14). Stylus.

Eidum, J., Lomicka, L., Chiang, W., Endick, G., & Stratton, J. (2020). Thriving in residential learning communities. *Learning Communities Research and Practice*, *8*(1), Article 7. https://washingtoncenter.evergreen.edu/lcrpjournal/vol8/iss1/7

Eli Review. (2016, August 3). Describe–evaluate–suggest: A helpful feedback pattern. *The Eli Review Blog*. https://elireview.com/2016/08/03/describe-evaluate-suggest/

Elon University Center for Writing Excellence. (n.d.). *Disciplinary writing consultants*. https://www.elon.edu/u/academics/writing-excellence/writing-across-the-university/writing-center-faculty-resources/disciplinary-writing-consultants/

English, F. W. (1978). *Quality control in curriculum development*. American Association of School Administrators.

English, F. W. (1980). Curriculum mapping. *Education Leadership, 37*(7), 558–559.

Epstein, I., Baljko, M., Thumlert, K., Kelly, E., Smith, J. A., Su, Y., Zaki-Azat, J., & May, N. M. (2020). "A video of myself helps me learn": A scoping review of the evidence of video-making for situated learning. *International Journal for the Scholarship of Teaching and Learning, 14*(1), Article 9. https://doi.org/10.20429/ijsotl.2020.140109

Eyler, J. S., Giles, D. E., Jr., Stenson, C. M., & Gray, C. J. (2001). *At a glance: What we know about the effects of service-learning on college students, faculty, institutions and communities, 1993–2000: Third edition.* Corporation for National Service, Learn and Serve America, and National Service Learning Clearinghouse.

Eynon, B., & Gambino, L. M. (2017). *High-impact ePortfolio practice: A catalyst for student, faculty, and institutional learning.* Stylus.

Eynon, B., & Gambino, L. M. (2018). Prologue. In B. Eynon & L. M. Gambino (Eds.), *Catalyst in action: Case studies of high-impact ePortfolio practice* (pp. xvii–xxxi). Stylus.

Farrell, A., Kane, S., Dube, C., & Salchak, S. (2017). Rethinking the role of higher education in college preparedness and success from the perspective of writing transfer. In J. L. Moore & R. Bass (Eds.), *Understanding writing transfer: Implications for transformative student learning in higher education* (pp. 81–92). Stylus.

Felten, P. (2017). Writing high-impact practices: Developing proactive knowledge in complex contexts. In J. L. Moore & R. Bass (Eds.), *Understanding writing transfer: Implications for transformative student learning in higher education* (pp. 49–58). Stylus.

Felten, P., Gardner, J. N., Schroeder, C. C., Lambert, L. M., & Barefoot, B. O. (2016). *The undergraduate experience: Focusing institutions on what matters most.* Jossey-Bass.

Felten, P., & Lambert, L. M. (2020). *Relationship-rich education: How human connections drive success in college.* Johns Hopkins University Press.

Fink, J., & Jenkins, D. (2021). Institutional barriers to baccalaureate transfer for community college students. In J. N. Gardner, M. J. Rosenberg, & A. K. Koch (Eds.), *The transfer experience: A handbook for creating a more equitable and successful postsecondary system* (pp. 29–49). Stylus.

Finley, A. (2021). *How college contributes to workforce success: Employer views on what matters most.* Association of American Colleges and Universities/Hanover Research. https://www.aacu.org/research/how-college-contributes-to-workforce-success

Finley, A., & McNair, T. (2013). *Assessing underserved students' engagement in high-impact practices.* Association of American Colleges and Universities.

Fleming, J., McLachlan, K., & Pretti, T. J. (2018). Successful work-integrated learning relationships: A framework for sustainability. *International Journal of Work-Integrated Learning, 19*(4), 321–335. https://www.ijwil.org/files/IJWIL_19_4_321_335.pdf

Fleming, J., Rowe, A. D., & Jackson, D. (2021). Employers as educators: The role of work placement supervisors in facilitating the transfer of skills and knowledge.

Journal of Education and Work, 34(5–6), 705–721. https://doi.org/10.1080/13639080.2021.1969343

Foster, J., & Yaoyuneyong, G. (2014). Collaborative cross-disciplinary client-based projects: A case study. *International Journal of Fashion Design, Technology and Education, 7*(3), 154–162. https://doi.org/10.1080/17543266.2014.937832

Fritsch, M. A., Culver, N., Culhane, N., Thigpen, J., & Lin, A. (2016). AdvoCaring: A cocurricular program to provide advocacy and caring to underserved populations in Baltimore. *American Journal of Pharmaceutical Education, 80*(7), Article 126. https://doi.org/10.5688/ajpe807126

Gardner, J. N., Rosenberg, M. J., & Koch, A. K. (Eds.). (2021). Introduction. In *The transfer experience: A handbook for creating a more equitable and successful postsecondary system* (pp. 1–11). Stylus.

Getman-Eraso, J., & Culkin, K. (2018). High-impact catalyst for success: ePortfolio integration in the first-year seminar. In B. Eynon & L. M. Gambino (Eds.), *Catalyst in action: Case studies of high-impact ePortfolio practice* (pp. 32–49). Stylus.

Gorzelsky, G., Hayes, C., Jones, E., & Driscoll, D. L. (2017). Cueing and adapting first-year writing knowledge: Support for transfer into disciplinary writing. In J. L. Moore & R. Bass (Eds.), *Understanding writing transfer: Implications for transformative student learning in higher education* (pp. 113–121). Stylus.

Gravett, S., de Beer, J., Odendaal-Kroon, R., & Merseth, K. K. (2017). The affordances of case-based teaching for the professional learning of student-teachers. *Journal of Curriculum Studies, 49*(3), 369–390. https://doi.org/10.1080/00220272.2016.1149224

Hall, E. A., Danielewicz, J., & Ware, J. (2013). Designs for writing: A metacognitive strategy for iterative drafting and revising. In M. Kaplan, N. Silver, D. Lavaque-Mantry, & D. Meizlish (Eds.), *Using reflection and metacognition to improve student learning* (pp. 147–170). Stylus.

Hall, E. E., Walkington, H., Shanahan, J. O., Ackley, E., & Stewart, K. A. (2018). Mentor perspectives on the place of undergraduate research mentoring in academic identity and career development: An analysis of award winning mentors. *International Journal of Academic Development, 23*(1), 15–27. https://doi.org/10.1080/1360144X.2017.1412972

Hansen, S. L. (2019). Using reflection to promote career-based learning in student employment. In A. Peck & K. Callahan (Eds.), *Leadership Development Through Campus Employment* (New Directions for Student Leadership, no. 162, pp. 61–73). Jossey-Bass. https://doi.org/10.1002/yd.20334

Hansen, S. L., & Hoag, B. A. (2018). Promoting learning, career readiness, and leadership in student employment. In K. K. Smith, G. S. Rooney, & G. Spencer (Eds.), *Leadership Development for Career Readiness in University Settings* (New Directions for Student Leadership, no. 157, pp. 85–99). Jossey-Bass. https://doi.org /10.1002/yd.20281

Hart-Davidson, W., & Graham Meeks, M. (2020). Feedback analytics for peer learning: Indicators of writing improvement in digital environments. In D. Kelly-Riley & N. Elliot (Eds.), *Improving outcomes: Disciplinary writing, local assessment, and the aim of fairness* (pp. 79–92). Modern Language Association.

Higher Education Quality Council of Ontario. (2016). *A practical guide for work-integrated learning: Effective practices to enhance the educational quality of structured work experiences offered through colleges and universities.* Queen's Printer for Ontario. https://heqco.ca/wp-content/uploads/2020/03/HEQCO_WIL_Guide_ENG_ACC.pdf

Hoffman, E. M. (2014). Faculty and student relationships: Context matters. *College Teaching, 62*(1), 13–19. https://doi.org/10.1080/87567555.2013.817379

Hussar, W. J., & Bailey, T. M. (2019). *Projections of education statistics to 2027.* National Center for Education Statistics.

Inkelas, K. K., Jessup-Anger, J., Benjamin, M., & Wawrzynski, M. (2018). *Living-learning communities that work: A research-based model for design, delivery, and assessment.* Stylus.

Inoue, A. B. (2004). Community-based assessment pedagogy. *Assessing Writing, 9*(3), 208–238. https://doi.org/10.1016/j.asw.2004.12.001

Jacoby, B. (2015). *Service-learning essentials: Questions, answers, and lessons.* Jossey-Bass.

Jenkins, D., & Fink, J. (2016). *Tracking transfer: New measures of institutional and state effectiveness in helping community college students attain bachelor's degrees.* Community College Research Center, Teachers College, Columbia University. https://ccrc.tc.columbia.edu/media/k2/attachments/tracking-transfer-institutional-state-effectiveness.pdf

Johnson, W. B. (2016). *On being a mentor: A guide for higher education faculty* (2nd ed.). Routledge.

Ketcham, C. J., Hall, E. E., Fitz Gibbon, H. M., & Walkington, H. (2018). Co-mentoring in undergraduate research: A faculty development perspective. In M. Vandermaas-Peeler, P. C. Miller, & J. L. Moore (Eds.), *Excellence in mentoring undergraduate research* (pp. 155–179). Council on Undergraduate Research.

Ketcham, C. J., Hall, E. E., & Miller, P. C. (2017). Co-mentoring undergraduate research: Student, faculty and institutional perspectives. *PURM: Perspectives of Undergraduate Research Mentoring, 6*(1), 1–13.

Ketcham, C. J., Moore, J. L., & Weaver, A. G. (2023). Conclusion: Committing to equitable, high-quality capstone experiences. In C. Ketcham, A. Weaver, & J. L. Moore (Eds.), *Cultivating capstones: Designing high-quality culminating experiences for student learning* (pp. 215–220). Stylus.

Ketcham, C. J., Weaver, A. G., Moore, J. L., & Felten, P. (2022). Living up to the capstone promise: Improving quality, equity, and outcomes in culminating experiences. In J. Zilvinskis, J. Kinzie, J. Daday, K. O'Donnell, & C. Vande Zande (Eds.), *Delivering on the promise of high-impact practices* (pp. 124–134). Stylus.

Kirkscey, R., Lewis, D. I., & Vale, J. (2023). Capstone influences and purposes. In C. Ketcham, A. Weaver, & J. L. Moore (Eds.), *Cultivating capstones: Designing high-quality culminating experiences for student learning* (pp. 41–53). Stylus.

Kiser, P. M. (1998). The integrative processing model: A framework for learning in the field experience. *Human Service Education, 18*(1), 3–13.

Kiser, P. M. (2014). *The human service internship: Getting the most from your experience* (4th ed.). Cengage.

Krain, M. (2016). Putting the learning in case learning? The effects of case-based approaches on student knowledge, attitudes, and engagement. *Journal on Excellence in College Teaching, 27*(2), 131–153.

Kuh, G. D. (2008). *High-impact educational practices: What they are, who has access to them, and why they matter.* Association of American Colleges and Universities.

Kuh, G. D. (2013). Taking HIPs to the next level. In G. D. Kuh & K. O'Donnell (Eds.), *Ensuring quality and taking high-impact practices to scale* (pp. 1–14). Association of American Colleges and Universities.

Kuh, G. D., Kinzie, J., Schuh, J. H., Whitt, E. J., & Associates. (2005). *Success in college: Creating conditions that matter.* Jossey-Bass.

Kuh, G. D., & O'Donnell, K. (2013). *Ensuring quality & taking high-impact practices to scale.* Association of American Colleges and Universities.

Kuh, G. D., O'Donnell, K., & Schneider, C. G. (2017). HIPs at ten. *Change: The Magazine of Higher Learning, 49*(5), 8–16. https://doi.org/10.1080/00091383.2017.1366805

Kunselman, J. C., & Johnson, K. A. (2004). Using the case method to facilitate learning. *College Teaching, 52*(3), 87–92. https://doi.org/10.3200/CTCH.52.3.87-92

Lambert, L., Husser, J., & Felten, P. (2018). Mentors play critical role in quality of college experience, new poll suggests. *The Conversation.* https://theconversation.com/mentors-play-critical-role-in-quality-of-college-experience-new-poll-suggests-101861

Lambert, P. (2003). Promoting developmental transfer in vocational teacher education. In T. Tuomi-Gröhn & Y. Engeström (Eds.), *Between school and work: New perspectives on transfer and boundary-crossing* (pp. 233–254). Emerald Group.

Lave, J., & Wenger, E. (1991). *Situated learning: Legitimate peripheral participation.* Cambridge University Press.

Layne, P., Glasco, S., Gillespie, J., Gross, D., & Jasinski, L. (2020). #Faculty-Matter: Faculty support and interventions integrated into global learning. In N. Namaste & A. Sturgill (Eds.), *Mind the gap: Global learning at home and abroad* (pp. 135–147). Stylus.

Levintova, E., Smith, S., Cruise, R., Berdrow, I., Boudon, L., Paracka, D., & Worley, P. M. (2020). Have interest, will *not* travel: Unexpected reasons why students opt out of international study. In N. Namaste & A. Sturgill (Eds.), *Mind the gap: Global learning at home and abroad* (pp. 122–134). Stylus.

Lewis, D. I., Bean, J., Beaudoin, C., Van Zile-Tamsen, C., & von der Heidt, T. (2023). Preparing students for the fourth industrial revolution. In C. Ketcham, A. Weaver, & J. L. Moore (Eds.), *Cultivating capstones: Designing high-quality culminating experiences for student learning* (pp. 85–97). Stylus.

Mackiewicz, J., & Thompson, I. (2014). Instruction, cognitive scaffolding, and motivational scaffolding in writing center tutoring. *Composition Studies, 42*(1), 54–78.

Magee, L., Hill, E. J. R., & Maile, E. J. (2012). Feedback delivery as a peer-tutor. *The Clinical Teacher, 9*, 56–57. https://doi.org/10.1111/j.1743-498X.2011.00502.x

Maltz, S., & Grahn, B. (2003). *A fork in the road: A career planning guide for young adults.* Impact Publications.

Manning, S., Frieders, Z., & Bikos, L. (2020). When does global learning begin: Recognizing the value of student experiences prior to study away. In N. Namaste & A. Sturgill (Eds.), *Mind the gap: Global learning at home and abroad* (pp. 43–54). Stylus.

Manz, J. W., Ward, M. D., & Gundlach, E. (2023). "Mine" the gap: Connecting curriculum, courses, and community. In J. E. Eidum & L. L. Lomicka (Eds.), *The faculty factor: Developing faculty engagement with living–learning communities* (pp. 147–161). Stylus.

Marshall, D. T., Love, S. M., & Scott, L. (2020). "It's not like he was being a robot": Student perceptions of video-based writing feedback in online graduate coursework. *International Journal for the Scholarship of Teaching and Learning, 14*(1), Article 10. https://doi.org/10.20429/ijsotl.2020.140110

McCabe, J. M. (2016). *Connecting in college: How friendship networks matter for academic and social success.* University of Chicago Press.

McCale, C. (2008). It's hard work learning soft skills: Can client based projects teach the soft skills students need and employers want? *Journal of Effective Teaching, 8*(2), 50–60.

McClellan, G. S., Creager, K., & Savoca, M. (2018). *A good job: Campus employment as a high-impact practice.* Stylus.

McCune, V., Tauritz, R., Boyd, S., Cross, A., Higgins, P., & Scoles, J. (2021, April 13). Teaching wicked problems in higher education: Ways of thinking and practicing. *Teaching in Higher Education.* Advance online publication. https://doi.org/10.1080/13562517.2021.1911986

McGrath, M. M., Dyer, S., Rankin, J., & Jorre de St. Jorre, T. (2023). Positionality and identity in capstones: Renegotiating the self through teaching and learning. In C. J. Ketcham, A. Weaver, & J. L. Moore (Eds.), *Cultivating capstones: Designing high-quality culminating experiences for student learning* (pp. 203–214). Stylus.

Meeks, M. (2016, November 10). Making a horse drink. *The Eli Review Blog.* https://elireview.com/2016/11/10/making-a-horse-drink/

Meeks, M. (2017, March 28). Giver's gain in peer learning. *The Eli Review Blog.* https://elireview.com/2017/03/28/givers-gain/

Micari, M., & Pazos, P. (2012). Connecting to the professor: Impacts of student–faculty relationship in a highly challenging course. *College Teaching, 60*(2), 41–47. https://doi.org/10.1080/87567555.2011.627576

Misyak, S., Culhane, J., McConnell, K., & Serrano, E. (2016). Assessment for learning: Integration of assessment in a nutrition course with a service-learning component. *NACTA Journal, 60*(4), 358–363.

Moore, D. T. (2013). *Engaged learning in the academy: Challenges and possibilities.* Palgrave MacMillan.

Moore, J. L. (2013). Preparing advocates: Service-learning in TESOL for future mainstream educators. *TESOL Journal, 4,* 555–570. https://doi.org/10.1002/tesj.97

Moore, J. L. (2017). Five essential principles about writing transfer. In J. L. Moore & R. Bass (Eds.), *Understanding writing transfer: Implications for transformative student learning in higher education* (pp. 1–12). Stylus.

Moore, J. L., Abbot, S., Bellwoar, H., & Watts, F. (2020). Mentoring: Partnering with all undergraduate researchers in writing. In D. DelliCarpini, J. Fishman, & J. Greer (Eds.), *The Naylor Report on undergraduate research in writing studies* (pp. 29–44). Parlor Press.

Moore, J. L., Pope-Ruark, R., & Strickland, M. (2018). Not just another assignment: Integrative ePortfolios, curricular integrity, and student professional identity. In B. Eynon & L. M. Gambino (Eds.), *Catalyst in action: Case studies of high-impact ePortfolio practice* (pp. 172–184). Stylus.

Mullin, J. (2001). Writing centers and WAC. In S. H. McLeod, E. Miraglia, M. Soven, & C. Thaiss (Eds.), *WAC for the new millennium: Strategies for continuing writing-across-the-curriculum programs* (pp. 179–199). National Council of Teachers of English.

Mutch, A., Young, C., Davey, T., & Fitzgerald, L. (2018). A journey towards sustainable feedback. *Assessment & Evaluation in Higher Education, 43*(2), 248–259. https://doi.org/10.1080/02602938.2017.1332154

Naegeli Costa, C., & Mims, L. C. (2021). Using notecard check-ins to build relationships and establish a climate of care. *College Teaching, 69*(1), 32–33. https://doi.org/10.1080/87567555.2020.1797619

National Academies of Sciences, Engineering, and Medicine. (2018). *How people learn II: Learners, contexts, and cultures*. The National Academies Press. https://doi.org/10.17226/24783

National Association of Colleges and Employers. (2021a). *2021 internship & co-op survey report: Executive summary.* https://www.naceweb.org/uploadedfiles/files/2021/publication/executive-summary/2021-nace-internship-and-co-op-survey-executive-summary.pdf

National Association of College and Employers. (2021b). *Composition of intern, co-op cohorts show employer DEI efforts are falling short.* https://www.naceweb.org/about-us/press/composition-of-intern-co-op-cohorts-show-employer-dei-efforts-are-falling-short/

National Association of Colleges and Employers. (2021c). *The 2020 student survey report: Attitudes and preferences of bachelor's degree students at four-year schools—Executive summary.* https://www.naceweb.org/uploadedfiles/files/2021/publication/executive-summary/2020-nace-student-survey-four-year-executive-summary.pdf

National Survey of Student Engagement. (n.d.). *High-impact practices.* NSSE Interactive Reports. https://tableau.bi.iu.edu/t/prd/views/ar20_hips/HIPsin2020

National Survey of Student Engagement. (2019a). *Engagement insights: Survey findings on the quality of undergraduate education—Annual results 2019.* https://hdl.handle.net/2022/25321

National Survey of Student Engagement. (2019b). *NSSE 2019 topical module report: Experiences with writing.* Indiana University Center for Postsecondary Research.

Nelms, G., & Dively, R. L. (2007). Perceived roadblocks to transferring knowledge from first-year composition to writing-intensive major courses: A pilot study. *Writing Program Administration, 31*(1–2), 214–240.

Nevison, C., Cormier, L., Pretti, T. J., & Drewery, D. (2018). The influence of values on supervisors' satisfaction with coop student employees. *International Journal of Work-Integrated Learning, 19*(1), 1–11. https://www.ijwil.org/files/IJWIL_19_1_1_11.pdf

Nicol, D. J., & Macfarlane-Dick, D. (2006). Formative assessment and self-regulated learning: A model and seven principles of good feedback practice. *Studies in Higher Education, 31*(2), 199–218. https://doi.org/10.1080/03075070600572090

Nkhoma, M., Sriratanaviriyakul, N., & Quang, H. L. (2017). Using case method to enrich students' learning outcomes. *Active Learning in Higher Education, 18*(1), 37–50. https://doi.org/10.1177/1469787417693501

Nowacek, R. S. (2011). *Agents of integration: Understanding transfer as a rhetorical act.* Southern Illinois University Press.

Open Doors. (2020). *Open Doors 2020 fast facts.* https://opendoorsdata.org/wp-content/uploads/2021/11/Fast-Facts-2010-2020.pdf

Palmer, R. J., Hunt, A. N., Neal, M. R., & Wuetherick, B. (2018). Mentored undergraduate research: An investigation into students' perceptions of its impact on identity development. In M. Vandermaas-Peeler, P. C. Miller, & J. L. Moore (Eds.), *Excellence in mentoring undergraduate research* (pp. 19–42). Council on Undergraduate Research.

Paras, A., & Mitchell, L. (2020). Up for the challenge? The role of disorientation and dissonance in intercultural learning. In N. Namaste & A. Sturgill (Eds.), *Mind the gap: Global learning at home and abroad* (pp. 96–108). Stylus.

Parks, R. L., & Hayes, C. (2019, November 15). Here's why your college should create learner profiles. *eCampus News.* https://www.ecampusnews.com/2019/11/15/heres-why-your-college-should-create-learner-profiles/

Perkins, D. N., & Salomon, G. (1988). Teaching for transfer. *Educational Leadership, 46*(1), 22–32.

Perkins, D. N., & Salomon, G. (1992). The science and art of transfer. In A. L. Costa, J. Bellanca, & R. Forgarty (Eds.), *If minds matter: A forward to the future* (Vol. 1, pp. 201–209). Skylight.

Pope-Ruark, R. (2012). We scrum every day: Using Scrum project management framework for group projects. *College Teaching, 60,* 164–169. https://doi.org/10.1080/87567555.2012.669425

Radhakrishnan, P., Hendrix, T., Mark, K., Taylor, B. J., & Veras, I. (2018). Building STEM identity with a core ePortfolio practice. In B. Eynon & L. M. Gambino (Eds.), *Catalyst in action: Case studies of high-impact ePortfolio practice* (pp. 223–240). Stylus.

Rajhans, V., Mohammed, C. A., Ve, R. S., & Prabhu, A. (2021). Revitalizing journal clubs: Millennial perspectives for enhancing student learning and engagement. *Education for Health: Change in Learning & Practice, 34*(1), 22–28. https://doi.org/10.4103/efh.EfH_69_20

Rathburn, M., Malmgren, J., Brenner, A., Carignan, M., Hardy, J., & Paras, A. (2020). Assessing intercultural competence in student writing: A multi-institutional study. In N. Namaste & A. Sturgill (Eds.), *Mind the gap: Global learning at home and abroad* (pp. 79–95). Stylus.

Renn, K. A., & Reason, R. D. (2021). *College students in the United States: Characteristics, experiences, and outcomes* (2nd ed.). Stylus.

Rittel, H. W. J., & Webber, M. M. (1973). Dilemmas in a general theory of planning. *Policy Sciences, 4*(2), 155–169. https://doi.org/10.1007/BF01405730

Robertson, L., & Taczak, K. (2017). Teaching for transfer. In J. L. Moore & R. Bass (Eds.), *Understanding writing transfer: Implications for transformative student learning in higher education* (pp. 93–102). Stylus.

Robinson, H. M., & Hall, J. (2013). Connecting WID and the writing center: Tools for collaboration. *The WAC Journal, 24,* 29–47. https://doi.org/10.37514/WAC-J .2013.24.1.02

Robley, W., Whittle, S., & Murdoch-Eaton, D. (2005). Mapping generic skills curricula: A recommended methodology. *Journal of Further and Higher Education, 29*(3), 221–231. https://doi.org/10.1080/03098770500166801

Rogers, C., & Andrews, V. (2016). Nonprofits' expectations in PR service-learning partnerships. *Journalism & Mass Communication Educator, 71*(1), 95–106. https://doi.org/10.1177/1077695815584226

Rosinski, P. (2016/2017). Students' perceptions of the transfer of rhetorical knowledge between digital self-sponsored writing and academic writing: The importance of authentic contexts and reflection. In C. A. Anson & J. L. Moore (Eds.), *Critical transitions: Writing and the question of transfer* (pp. 247–271). The WAC Clearinghouse/University Press of Colorado. https://doi.org/10.37514/ PER-B.2016.0797.2.09

Sadika, B., Soubry, I., Kleiboer, B., Aubry-Wake, C., Toop, F., Leonhardt, R., Lindsay, R., & Massie, M. (2022). The first year research experience (FYRE): Through the eyes of research coaches. *Perspectives on Undergraduate Research & Mentoring, 10*(1). https://eloncdn.blob.core.windows.net/eu3/sites/923/2022/02/ Sadika-et-al_T2110.pdf

Sadler, D. R. (1989). Formative assessment and the design of instructional systems. *Instructional Science, 18,* 119–144. https://doi.org/10.1007/BF00117714

Salomon, G., & Perkins, D. N. (1989). Rocky roads to transfer: Rethinking mechanism of a neglected phenomenon. *Educational Psychologist, 24*(2), 113–142. https://doi.org/10.1207/s15326985ep2402_1

Sandefur, C. I., & Gordy, C. (2016). Undergraduate journal club as an intervention to improve student development in applying the scientific process. *Journal of College Science Teaching, 45*(4), 52–58. https://doi.org/10.2505/4/ jcst16_045_04_52

Schön, D. A. (1983). *The reflective practitioner: How professionals think in action.* Basic Books.

Schreiner, L. A. (2016). Thriving: Expanding the goal of higher education. In D. W. Harward (Ed.), *Well-being and higher education: A strategy for change and the realization of education's greater purpose* (pp. 135–148). American Association of Colleges and Universities.

Schwartz, D. L., Tsang, J. M., & Blair, K. P. (2016). *The ABCs of how we learn: 26 scientifically proven approaches, how they work, and when to use them.* Norton.

Shanahan, J. O. (2018). Mentoring strategies that support underrepresented students in undergraduate research. In M. Vandermaas-Peeler, P. C. Miller, & J. L. Moore (Eds.), *Excellence in mentoring undergraduate research* (pp. 43–75). Council on Undergraduate Research.

Shanahan, J. O., Ackley-Holbrook, E., Hall, E., Stewart, K., & Walkington, H. (2015). Ten salient practices of undergraduate research mentors: A review of the literature. *Mentoring and Tutoring: Partnership in Learning, 5*, 359–376. http://doi.org/10.1080/13611267.2015.1126162

Shanahan, J. O., Walkington, H., Ackley, E., Hall, E., & Stewart, K. (2017). Award-winning mentors see democratization as the future of undergraduate research. *CUR Quarterly, 37*(4), 4–11. https://doi.org/10.18833/curq/37/4/14

Shin, J., Kim, M., Hwang, H., & Lee, B. (2018). Effectives of intrinsic motivation and informative feedback in service-learning on the development of college students' life purpose. *Journal of Moral Education, 47*(2), 159–174. https://doi.org/10.1080/03057240.2017.1419943

Silver, N. (2013). Reflective pedagogies and the metacognitive turn in college teaching. In M. Kaplan, N. Silver, D. Lavaque-Mantry, & D. Meizlish (Eds.), *Using reflection and metacognition to improve student learning* (pp. 1–17). Stylus.

Simonsmeier, B. A., Peiffer, H., Flaig, M., & Schneider, M. (2020). Peer feedback improves students' academic self-concept in higher education. *Research in Higher Education, 61*, 706–724. https://doi.org/10.1007/s11162-020-09591-y

Smith, T. (2008). Integrating undergraduate peer mentors into liberal arts courses: A pilot study. *Innovative Higher Education, 33*(1), 49–63. https://doi.org/10.1007/s10755-007-9064-6

Soven, M. (2001). Curriculum-based peer tutors and WAC. In S. H. McLeod, E. Miraglia, M. Soven, & C. Thaiss (Eds.), *WAC for the new millennium: Strategies for continuing writing-across-the-curriculum programs* (pp. 200–232). National Council of Teachers of English.

Sriram, R., Haynes, C., Cheatle, J., Marquart, C. P., Murray, J. L., & Weintraub, S. D. (2020). The development and validation of an instrument measuring academic, social, and deeper life interactions. *Journal of College Student Development, 61*, 240–245. https://doi.org/10.1353/csd.2020.0020

Sriram, R., Haynes, C., Weintraub, S. D., Cheatle, J., Marquart, C. P., & Murray, J. L. (2020). Student demographics and experiences of deeper life interactions within residential learning communities. *Learning Communities Research and Practice, 8*(1), Article 8. https://washingtoncenter.evergreen.edu/lcrpjournal/vol8/iss1/8

Sriram, R., Weintraub, S. D., Cheatle, J., Haynes, C., Murray, J. L., & Marquart, C. P. (2020). The influence of academic, social, and deeper life interactions on students' psychological sense of community. *Journal of College Student Development, 61*(5), 593–608. https://doi.org/10.1353/csd.2020.0057

Stommel, J. (2020). How to ungrade. In S. D. Blum (Ed.), *Ungrading: Why rating students undermines learning (and what to do instead)* (pp. 25–41). West Virginia University Press.

Stovner, R. B., Klette, K., & Nortvedt, G. A. (2021). The instructional situations in which mathematics teachers provide substantive feedback. *Educational Studies in Mathematics, 108*, 533–551. https://doi.org/10.1007/s10649-021-10065-w

Stuckey, M., Waggoner, Z., & Erdem, E. (2018). Writing and reflecting for transfer: Using high-impact ePortfolios in online first-year composition. In B. Eynon & L. M. Gambino (Eds.), *Catalyst in action: Case studies of high-impact ePortfolio practice* (pp. 113–124). Stylus.

Sturgill, A. (2020). Crossing borders at home: The promise of global learning close to campus. In N. Namaste & A. Sturgill (Eds.), *Mind the gap: Global learning at home and abroad* (pp. 70–78). Stylus.

Sullivan, W. M. (2016). *The power of integrated learning: Higher education for success in life, work, and society.* Stylus.

Swaner, L., & Brownell, J. (2008). *Outcomes of high-impact practices for underserved students: A review of the literature.* Association of American Colleges and Universities.

Thistlethwaite, J. E., Davies, D., Ekeocha, S., Kidd, J. M., MacDougall, C., Matthews, P., Purkis, J., & Clay, D. (2012). The effectiveness of case-based learning in health professional education. A BEME systematic review (BEME Guide No. 23). *Medical Teacher, 34*(6), e421–e444. https://doi.org/10.3109/0142159X.2012.680939

Tofighi, M. (2021). Differential effect of client-based and non-client-based projects on marketing students' course performance and evaluations. *Marketing Education Review*, 1–17. https://doi.org/10.1080/10528008.2021.1871851

Tuomi-Gröhn, T., Engeström, Y., & Young, M. (2003). From transfer to boundary-crossing between school and work as a tool for developing vocational education: An introduction. In T. Tuomi-Gröhn & Y. Engeström (Eds.), *Between school and work: New perspectives on transfer and boundary-crossing* (pp. 1–15). Emerald Group.

UB Curriculum. (n.d.). *UB portfolio: A purposeful digital collection of your work.* https://www.buffalo.edu/ubcurriculum/capstone/ubportfolio.html

University of Iowa Division of Student Life. (n.d.). *Iowa Grow®.* https://studentlife.uiowa.edu/initiatives/iowa-grow®/

University of South Carolina. (n.d.). *GLD ePortfolio content guide.* https://sc.edu/about/initiatives/center_for_integrative_experiential_learning/documents/gld_documents/2021_gld_eportfolio_content_guide.pdf

Vale, J., Gordon, K., Kirkscey, R., & Hill, J. (2020). Student and faculty perceptions of capstone purposes: What can engineering learn from other disciplines? *Proceedings of the Canadian Engineering Education Association (CEEA) Conference, 2020*, 1–8. https://doi.org/10.24908/pceea.vi0.14149

Van Scoy, I. J., Fallucca, A., Harrison, T., & Camp, L. D. (2018). Integrative learning and graduation with leadership distinction: ePortfolios and institutional change. In B. Eynon & L. M. Gambino (Eds.), *Catalyst in action: Case studies of high-impact ePortfolio practice* (pp. 15–31). Stylus.

Van Zile-Tamsen, C., Bean, J., Beaudoin, C., Lewis, D. I., & von der Heidt, T. (2023). Where there's a will, there's a way: Implementing a capstone experience for general education. In C. Ketcham, A. Weaver, & J. L. Moore (Eds.), *Cultivat-*

ing capstones: Designing high-quality culminating experiences for student learning (pp. 73–82). Stylus.

Veltman, M. E., Van Keulen, J., & Voogt, J. M. (2019). Design principles for addressing wicked problems through boundary crossing in higher professional education. *Journal of Education and Work, 32*(2), 135–155. https://doi.org/10 .1080/13639080.2019.1610165

Walkington, H., Hall, E., Shanahan, J. O., Ackley, E., & Stewart, K. (2018). Striving for excellence in undergraduate research mentoring: The challenges and approaches to ten salient practices. In M. Vandermaas-Peeler, P. C. Miller, & J. L. Moore (Eds), *Excellence in mentoring undergraduate research* (pp. 105–129). Council on Undergraduate Research.

Wardle, E., & Mercer Clement, N. (2016/2017). Double binds and consequential transitions: Considering matters of identity during moments of rhetorical challenge. In C. A. Anson & J. L. Moore (Eds.), *Critical transitions: Writing and the question of transfer* (pp. 161–179). The WAC Clearinghouse/University Press of Colorado. https://doi.org/10.37514/PER-B.2016.0797.2.06

Wardle, E., & Mercer Clement, N. (2017). "The hardest thing with writing is not getting enough instruction": Helping educators guide students through writing challenges. In J. L. Moore & R. Bass (Eds.), *Understanding writing transfer: Implications for transformative student learning in higher education* (pp. 131–143). Stylus.

Watling, C., Driessen, E., van der Vleuten, C. P. M., & Lingard, L. (2014). Learning culture and feedback: An international study of medical athletes and musicians. *Medical Education, 48*, 713–723. https://doi.org/10.1111/medu.12407

Weissbach, R. S., & Pflueger, R. C. (2018). Collaborating with writing centers on interdisciplinary peer tutor training to improve writing support for engineering students. *IEEE Transactions on Professional Communication, 61*(2), 206–220. https://doi.org/ 10.1109/TPC.2017.2778949

Wilson, W. L., & Arendale, D. R. (2011). Peer educators in learning assistance programs: Best practices for new programs. In L. B. Williams (Ed.), *Emerging Issues and Practices in Peer Education* (New Directions for Student Services, no. 133, pp. 41–53). Jossey-Bass. https://doi.org/10.1002/ss.383

Winstone, N., & Carless, D. (2020). *Designing effective feedback processes in higher education: A learning-focused approach.* Routledge.

Wolf-Wendel, L., Ward, K., & Kinzie, J. (2009). A tangled web of terms: The overlap and unique contribution of involvement, engagement, and integration to understanding college student success. *Journal of College Student Development, 50*(4), 407–428.

World Economic Forum. (2020). *The future of jobs report 2020.* https://www3 .weforum.org/docs/WEF_Future_of_Jobs_2020.pdf

Wuetherick, B., Willison, J., & Shanahan, J. O. (2018). Mentored undergraduate research at scale: Undergraduate research in the curriculum and as pedagogy. In M. Vandermaas-Peeler, P. C. Miller, & J. L. Moore (Eds.), *Excellence in mentoring undergraduate research* (pp. 181–202). Council on Undergraduate Research.

Yancey, K. B. (1998). *Reflection in the writing classroom.* University Press of Colorado/Utah State University Press. https://doi.org/10.2307/j.ctt46nsh0

Yancey, K. B. (2017). Writing, transfer, and ePortfolios: A possible trifecta in supporting student learning. In J. L. Moore & R. Bass (Eds.), *Understanding writing transfer: Implications for transformative student learning in higher education* (pp. 39–48). Stylus.

Yancey, K. B., Robertson, L., & Taczak, K. (2014). *Writing across contexts: Transfer, composition, and sites of writing.* Utah State University Press.

ABOUT THE AUTHOR

Jessie L. Moore, PhD, is director of the Center for Engaged Learning and professor of English: professional writing and rhetoric at Elon University. Jessie leads planning, implementation, and assessment of the center's research seminars, which support multi-institutional inquiry on high-impact pedagogies and other focused engaged learning topics. Her recent research examines high-impact pedagogies, the writing lives of university students and recent college graduates, multi-institutional research and collaborative inquiry, and writing residencies for faculty writers. She has coedited several engaged learning books, including *Cultivating Capstones: Designing High-Quality Culminating Experiences for Student Learning* (with Caroline J. Ketcham and Anthony G. Weaver; Stylus, 2023), *Excellence in Mentoring Undergraduate Research* (with Maureen Vandermaas-Peeler and Paul Miller; CUR, 2018), and *Understanding Writing Transfer: Implications for Transformative Student Learning in Higher Education* (with Randy Bass; Stylus, 2017). In 2019, Jessie's professional service to the scholarship of teaching and learning was recognized with the International Society for the Scholarship of Teaching and Learning Distinguished Service Award, and in 2021, Jessie received Elon University's Distinguished Scholar Award.

The Center for Engaged Learning at Elon University (www .CenterForEngagedLearning.org) brings together international leaders in higher education to develop and to synthesize rigorous research on central questions about student learning.

Researchers have identified "high-impact" educational practices—undergraduate research, internships, service-learning, writing-intensive courses, study abroad, living-learning communities, and so on. While we know *what* these practices are, we could know much more about three essential issues:

- *how* to do these practices well and in diverse contexts,
- how to *scale* these practices equitably to all students, and
- how students *integrate* their learning across multiple high impact experiences.

The Center for Engaged Learning fosters investigations of these and related questions, principally by hosting multi-institutional research and practice-based initiatives, conferences, and seminars. All of this work attends to diversity, inclusion, access, and equity in engaged learning. To date, more than 200 scholars from over 120 postsecondary institutions across more than a dozen countries on five continents have participated in the center's research seminars, focusing on topics like mentoring undergraduate research, global learning, residential learning, capstone experiences, and preparing students for writing beyond the university.

The Center also develops open-access resources on engaged learning practices and research for faculty and educational developers. Thousands of visitors engage with these resources each month, with readers accessing the site from around the globe (over 190 countries and counting). Visit www .CenterForEngagedLearning.org to access supplemental resources for books in this series, as well as weekly blog posts, podcast episodes, videos, and introductory resource guides both on specific engaged learning topics and on strategies for pursuing scholarship of teaching and learning.

Jessie L. Moore
Director
jmoore28@elon.edu

Peter Felten
Executive Director
pfelten@elon.edu